MW01631115

BETTER ELECTRIC LAMPS OF THE 20'S & 30'S.

Moe Bridges, Pittsburgh, and others.

Edited by
L-W Book Sales

Published By:
L-W Book Sales
P.O. Box 69
Gas City, IN 46933

ISBN#: 0-89538-087-0

Published by: L-W Book Sales
P.O. Box 69
Gas City, IN 46933

Please write for our free catalog.

Printed by IMAGE GRAPHICS, INC., Paducah, Kentucky

TABLE OF CONTENTS

INTRODUCTION

This book has been compiled from original catalogs owned by L-W Book Sales. The lamps illustrated within will assure the collector and dealer of perfect matches on shades and bases. We feel that this book will be a great tool for identifying these lamps.

PRICING INFORMATION

The enclosed price guide is of current market values. In some regions of the country the prices will vary. You must remember that this is only a guide and meant to be used as such. We are not responsible for any loss or gain of money from selling or buying of lamps. This is only a price guide to assist you in getting a general idea of the prices.

Remember, every time a lamp is sold at auction, a 10% to 15% buyer's premium is added. This alone is causing the price of better lamps to raise considerably.

Here is a list of some of the Collectors, Dealers, and Restorers of Lamps throughout the country.

Cincinnati Art Gallery-635 Main St., Cincinnati, OH 45202
Garth's Auction Inc.-Box 369, Delaware, OH 43015
David Kurtz-Urbana, IL 61801
McAllister Auction Service-958 Maynard Rd., Portland, MI 48875
Prater's Auction Service-50600 St.Rt. 14 Unity, East Palestine, OH 44413
Don Treadway Gallery-2128 Madison Rd., Cincinnati, OH 45208
Chris Olah/Century Antiques-7410 Lorain, Cleveland, OH 44102
Edward Malakoff/Pairpoint Lamp Musuem-276 Princeton Dr., River Edge, NJ 07661
House of Anteiks-4008 College, Synder, TX 79549
James Roush/Antiques Ltd.-739 W. 5th St., Marion, IN 46952

MOE-BRIDGES COMPANY
Lighting Equipment

B-95
Finish, Italian Polychrome
Height, 64 inches
Canopy Switch

Moe-Bridges Artistic Lighting Equipment

PORTABLE Lighting Equipment, such as that illustrated in the succeeding pages, meets a definite requirement in the furnishing of the home.

As a complement to the Lighting Fixtures, its function is to provide illumination and to contribute decorative harmony and beauty to its surroundings.

Acknowledged to be one of the largest and most successful manufacturers in this field, the Moe-Bridges Company is well qualified to design and build Lighting Fixtures and Portable Lighting Equipment that will harmonize with prevalent decorative requirements.

In designing, manufacturing and finishing the Portable Artistic Lighting Equipment herein illustrated, the highest standards of artistry have been adhered to.

No product leaves our Factory without our Guarantee Tag attached thereto — no Guarantee Tag is attached until we have done our very best!

Because of our exacting standards you can buy Moe-Bridges Lighting Equipment confident in the knowledge that it will contribute generously to the attractiveness of your home and that it will serve you to your whole-hearted satisfaction.

MOE-BRIDGES COMPANY

"Decorate with Artistic Lighting Equipment"

B-95
Finish, Italian Polychrome
Height, 64 inches
Canopy Switch

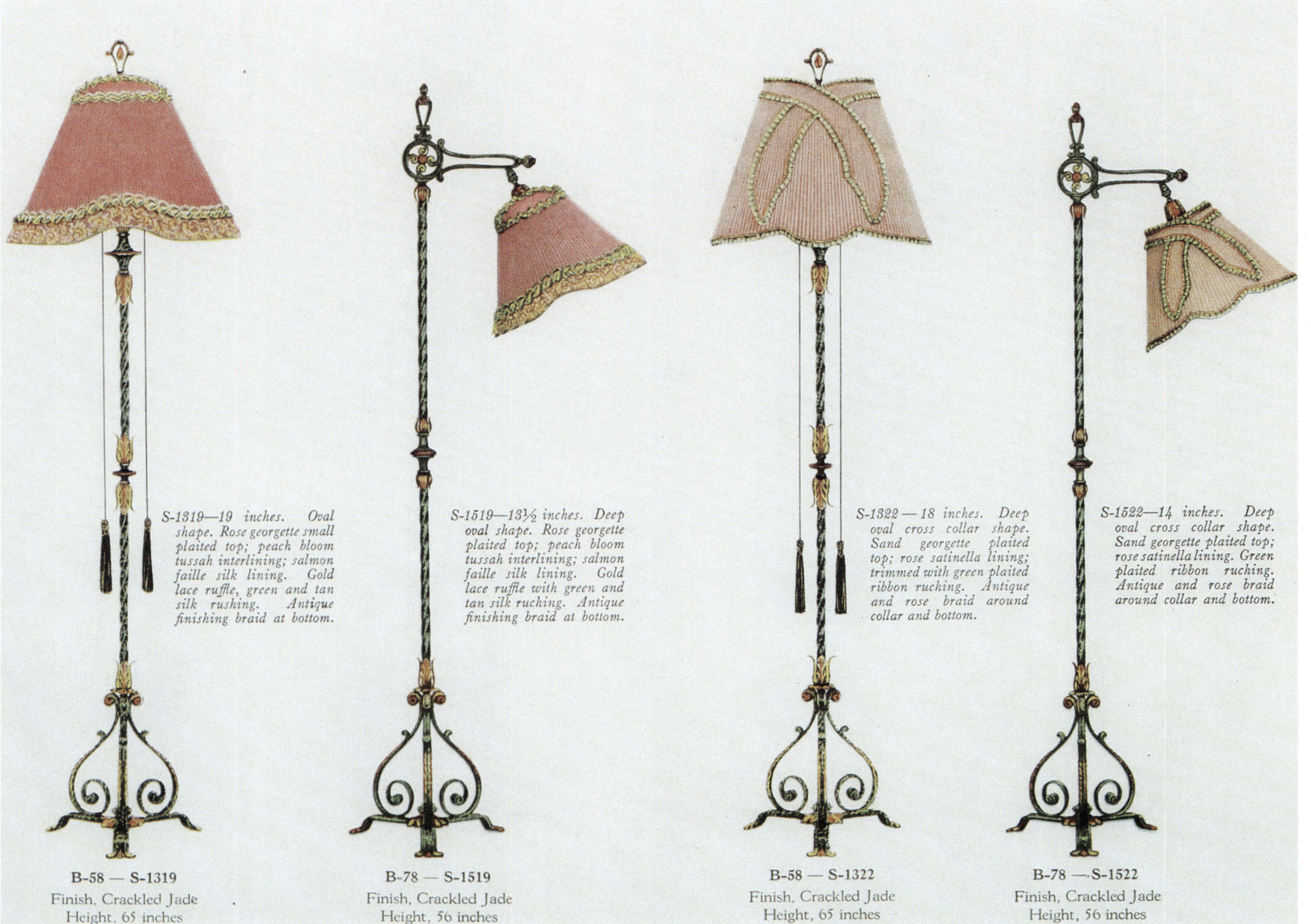

S-1319—19 inches. Oval shape. Rose georgette small plaited top; peach bloom tussah interlining; salmon faille silk lining. Gold lace ruffle, green and tan silk rushing. Antique finishing braid at bottom.

B-58 — S-1319
Finish, Crackled Jade
Height, 65 inches

S-1519—13½ inches. Deep oval shape. Rose georgette plaited top; peach bloom tussah interlining; salmon faille silk lining. Gold lace ruffle with green and tan silk ruching. Antique finishing braid at bottom.

B-78 — S-1519
Finish, Crackled Jade
Height, 56 inches

S-1322 — 18 inches. Deep oval cross collar shape. Sand georgette plaited top; rose satinella lining; trimmed with green plaited ribbon ruching. Antique and rose braid around collar and bottom.

B-58 — S-1322
Finish, Crackled Jade
Height, 65 inches

S-1522—14 inches. Deep oval cross collar shape. Sand georgette plaited top; rose satinella lining. Green plaited ribbon ruching. Antique and rose braid around collar and bottom.

B-78 — S-1522
Finish, Crackled Jade
Height, 56 inches

S-1306 — 16 inches. Deep round cone shape. Black georgette, small plaited top. Gold tussah interlining; peach changeable taffetone lining. Hand made ruching of antique metallic cloth, picot edged in black with fancy ruching in center. Flower trim applied.

B-52 — S-1306
Finish, Antique Gold
Height, 65 inches

S-1301—16 inches. Deep oval shape. Taupe georgette, small plaited top. Rose taffetex interlining with honeydew radium silk lining. Hand made ruching of taupe georgette with gold lace edging; variegated cord in center flower trim.

B-52 — S-1301
Finish, Jade and Gold
Height, 65 inches

S-1305 — 20 inches. Flat round shape. Putty georgette plaited top; orange Satinella interlining; burnt orange Jap silk lining. Double six inch putty fringe; ornate silk and antique band. Hand made two-tone ruching on collar.

B-53 — S-1305
Finish, Polychrome
Height, 65 inches

S-1302 — 19 inches. Deep round scalloped shape. Beaver georgette plaited top; rose tussah interlining; gold tussah lining. Polychrome and antique ruching.

B-55 — S-1302
Finish, Italian Polychrome
Height, 64 inches

S-1718—14 inches. Round cone shape. Cat tail georgette small plaited top. Peach bloom taffetex interlining. Honeydew twill silk lining. Shaded light green and peach ribbon at top and bottom. Fancy pastel pointed braid in center.

B-32 — S-1718
Finish, Venetian Gold
Height, 28 inches

B-31 — S-1254
Hand Wrought Base
Finish Swedish Iron
Height 20⅝ inches
Pull Chain Sockets
Oval Parchment Shade
14 inches extreme diameter
Black and Gold Braid Edging

S-1716—Round cone shape. Imported Spring Garden Glazed Chintz. Opaque black background; natural colored Spring flowers. Gold satin taffeta ribbon binding, top and bottom. Sunproof.

B-32 — S-1716
Finish, Venetian Gold
Height 28 inches

B-27 — S-1201-A
Finish, Hammered Brass
Height, 29 inches
Pull Chain Sockets
Oval Parchment Shade

B-30 — S-1255
Finish, Colonial Brass
Height, 22½ inches
Round Cone Parchment, bottom diameter, 6 inches
Canopy Switch

S-1714 — 18 inches. Oval Shape. Putty georgette plaited top. Yellow Satinella interlining. Burnt orange tub silk lining; antique and black silk pointed braid.

B-27 — S-1714
Finish, Swedish Iron
Height, 29 inches
Pull Chain Sockets

S-1716—Round shape. Imported Spring Garden Glazed Chintz. Opaque black background; natural colored Spring flowers. Gold satin taffeta ribbon binding, top and bottom. Sunproof.

B-29 — S-1716
Finish, Italian Polychrome
Height, 25 inches

S-1713—15 inches. Round scalloped frame. Parrot radium silk plaited top. Pink radium silk lining; polychrome ruching. Piped with black velvet ribbon.

B-29 — S-1713
Finish, Italian Polychrome
Height, 25 inches

S-1715—Round cone. Imported Glazed Chintz. Henna and brown with touches of blue and salmon; design outlined in black. Black satin taffeta ribbon binding, top and bottom. Sunproof and Waterproof for cleaning.

B-29 — S-1715
Finish, Italian Polychrome
Height, 25 inches

S-1802—Deep scalloped oval shape. Orchid georgette shirred top, orange lining. Orchid and purple bud braid. Ruffle at bottom. Floral cluster on plain panel.

B-5 — S-1802
Finish, Ivory Polychrome
Height, 13 inches

S-1801—Deep oval shape, Peach georgette shirred top. Orange lining. Trimmed with blue and gold bud braid with ruffle at bottom.

B-5 — S-1801
Finish, Ivory Polychrome
Height, 13 inches

S-1804—Oval shape. Putty georgette shirred top. Orange lining. Black and antique wide braid at top and bottom.

B-5 — S-1804
Finish, Rustic Gold Polychrome
Height, 13 inches

S-1803 — Round scalloped bottom shape. Turquoise blue georgette shirred top. Orange lining. Pink and gold braid. Ruffle at bottom.

B-5 — S-1803
Finish, Ivory Polychrome
Height, 13 inches

B-5 — S-1250
Finish, Rustic Gold Polychrome
Height, 12 inches
Oval Batik Shade

B-5 — S-1251
Finish, Rustic Gold Polychrome
Height, 12 inches
Oval Parchment Shade

ALL lamps are equipped with six feet of silk cord in colors to harmonize with the base.

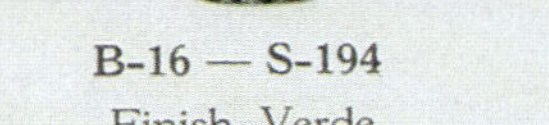

S-194—In this shade the Artist has caught the glories of the Athenian skies casting a flood of soft light like a mantle, myriad colored, round the ruins of the Parthenon at Athens. The blue sky melting into a golden streak of pale yellow finds its reflection in waters of the Ilissus, and is mirrored back to shore, bringing out in soft relief the purple mountains and the villages nestled at the base, where lived the dependents of some Athenian Prince.

B-16 — S-194
Finish, Verde
Height, 23 inches
Shade, 18 inches

S-192—An Autumnal Sunset. Let your imagination carry you along the country byway as it winds in and out among the silent sentinels of this woodland to the clear sparkling pool that lies beyond. Such a scene beckons you to peaceful meditation and refreshing rest.

B-19 — S-192
Finish, Crackled Green and Gold
Height, 23 inches
Shade, 18 inches

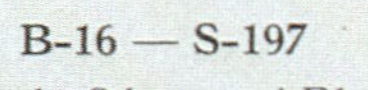

S-184—The "Flight of the Geese" is an artistic study of such unusual color effects, so startling and pleasing in its originality, that one is spell-bound under the inspiration of its mystic charm. Startled from their haunt, the wild geese wing their silent flight over the water, stand for a moment like silhouettes against the silver moon, then soar above the black hills of the opposite shore from which six stately pines raise their lofty heads into the red of the evening sky.

B-14 — S-184
Finish, Ebony and Gold
Height, 23 inches
Shade, 18 inches

S-197—This shade depicts a winter sunset in the snow clad mountains. Two evergreens lift their trunks aloft and stand out in strong relief against the white of the snow-covered ground and the waters of the lake. The border of black trees at the base of the snow-capped mountains accentuates their majesty and makes the white sunset shine upon their peaks in glorious splendor. This shade calls one to reverent reveries.

B-16 — S-197
Finish, Silver and Blue
Height, 23 inches
Shade, 18 inches

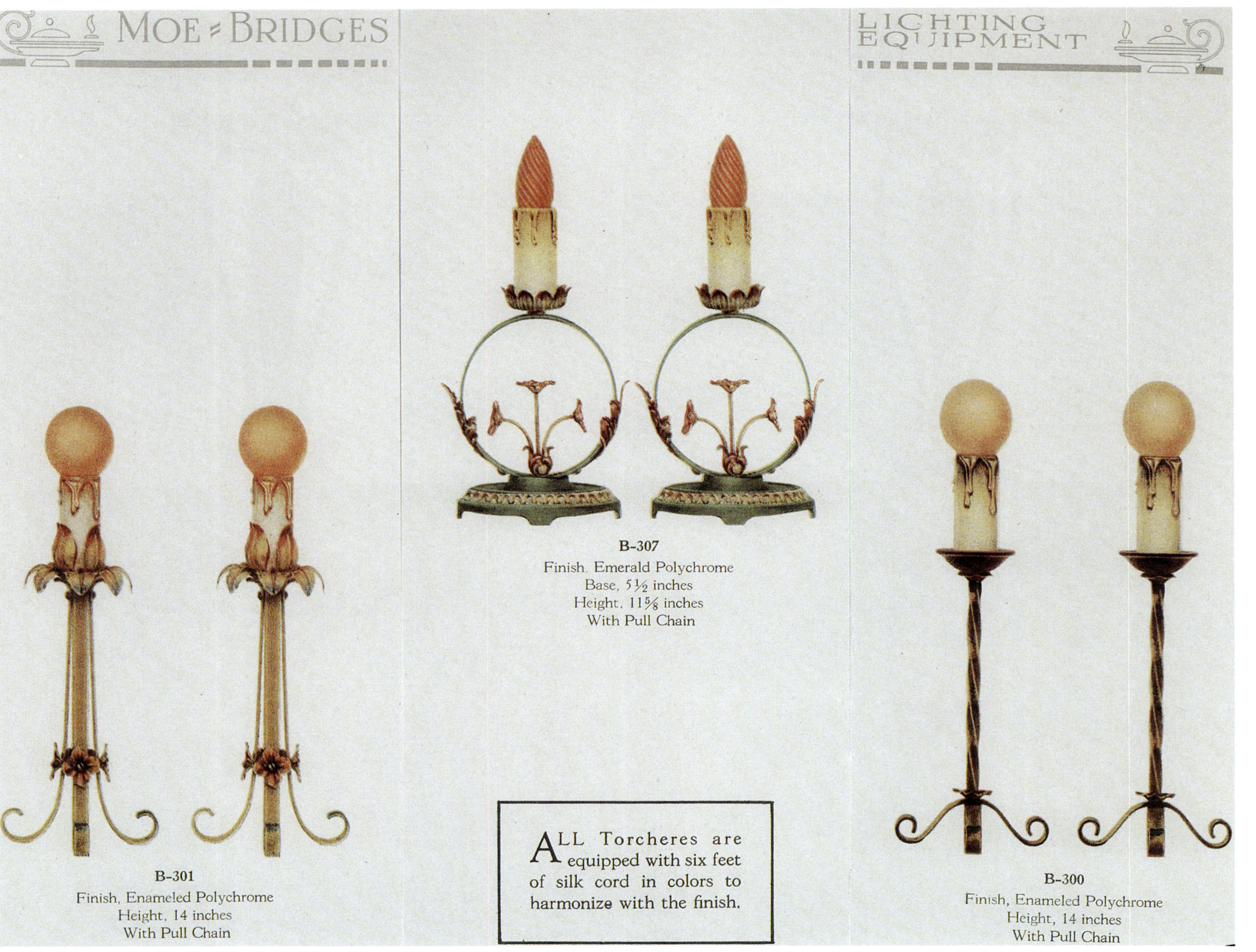

MOE = BRIDGES

LIGHTING EQUIPMENT

B-301
Finish, Enameled Polychrome
Height, 14 inches
With Pull Chain

B-307
Finish, Emerald Polychrome
Base, 5½ inches
Height, 11⅝ inches
With Pull Chain

ALL Torcheres are equipped with six feet of silk cord in colors to harmonize with the finish.

B-300
Finish, Enameled Polychrome
Height, 14 inches
With Pull Chain

MOE-BRIDGES

LIGHTING EQUIPMENT

S-188—Under a summer sky of blue, these beautiful Birds of Paradise with their red breasts, yellow wings and marvelous, filmy tails, are perched on a limb facing each other, proudly adding their beauty to this tropic scene. The palms and butterflies, the browns and greens of the base are welded into tropical surroundings of great beauty for our feathered friends. This shade affords ample light, is extremely cheerful and destined to be in great demand.

B-17 — S-188
Finish, Gold Polychrome
Height, 23 inches
Shade, 18 inches

S-202—Wild Roses, it seems, delight to perfume the air and brighten otherwise somber surroundings. This happy characteristic is given expression by the artist in his exquisite handling of the subject on this shade. Buds are fairly bursting with joy in their eagerness to be in full bloom and spread their fragrance and their beauty.

B-17 — S-202
Finish, Polychrome
Height, 23 inches
Shade, 18 inches

S-190—One must see this shade to appreciate how truly our Artist held the mirror up to nature in the execution of his work. Yellows, pinks, greens and browns are delicately blended in this work of art. The ruby red in the Chrysanthemums at the base mingle with these colors that fade into a light yellow, green and gold at the top in which are set two delicate pink blossoms in full bloom. The effect is truly wonderful.

B-18 — S-190
Finish, Crackled Gold
Height, 23 inches
Shade, 18 inches

S-201—Like a mirror in a golden frame, this clear, sparkling stream, winding its lazy way through meadowland, reflects the foliage that graces its course, and the evening sky above. Reveries carry one to the crest of the bridge, there to gaze down at the reflection of one who is thankful for the restfulness and peace that is to be found amid such settings as Nature alone can provide.

B-17 — S-201
Finish, Silver Polychrome
Height, 23 inches
Shade, 18 inches

S-251—A rarely traversed country road winding through fields in which grasses, shrubs and trees are rejoicing that spring-time has again called them back to life. A pleasant road to roam when time is plentiful and the love of the outdoors urges. A pleasant scene to view when rest and relaxation will gladden a tired body.

B-28 — S-251
Finish, Emerald Polychrome
Height, 23 inches
Shade, 15 inches

S-254—A bowl, overflowing with Nasturtiums just recently gathered from the garden, is a most refreshing thing to behold. So varied in color are the flowers—orange, scarlets, crimsons—blending from intensely vivid tones to soft, delicate tints. It is evident by this beautiful portrayal that the artist who paints this shade is a lover of flowers, and particularly, of Nasturtiums.

B-28 — S-254
Finish, Rustic Polychrome
Height, 23 inches
Shade, 15 inches

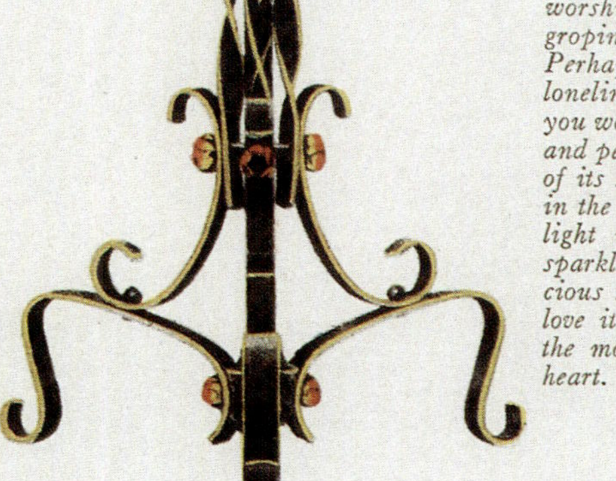

S-255 — A lovely country road, skirting a placid mountain lake. At its end, the village house of worship, with its spire groping toward the skies. Perhaps you would fear the loneliness of the spot. But you would love its quietude and peacefulness; the glory of its setting sun, reflected in the hill-enclosed lake as light is reflected from a sparkling stone in a precious setting. You would love its starlit nights and the moon that warms the heart.

B-28 — S-255
Finish, Ebony and Gold
Height, 23 inches
Shade, 15 inches

S-166—A MIDSUMMER Sunset, casting its fiery glow over trees and shrubbery and the placid pool which these surround. The spell of the evening's quiet pervades Nature's earthly possessions—all is calm and peaceful — awaiting the vanguard of the starry host that will soon dot the evening sky.

B-20 — S-166
Finish, Ebony and Gold
Height, 20 inches
Shade, 15 inches

B-3 — S-11
Finish, Silver and Blue
Height, 13 inches
Shade, 8 inches

B-3 — S-13
Finish, Ivory
Height, 13 inches
Shade, 8 inches

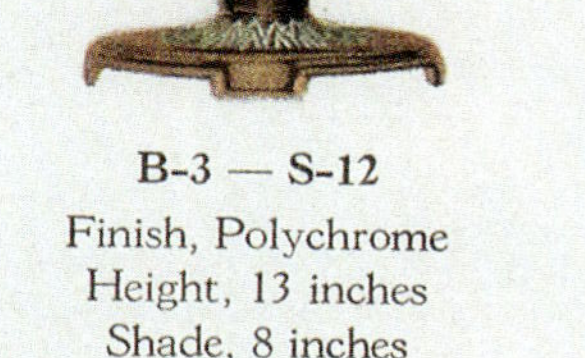

B-3 — S-12
Finish, Polychrome
Height, 13 inches
Shade, 8 inches

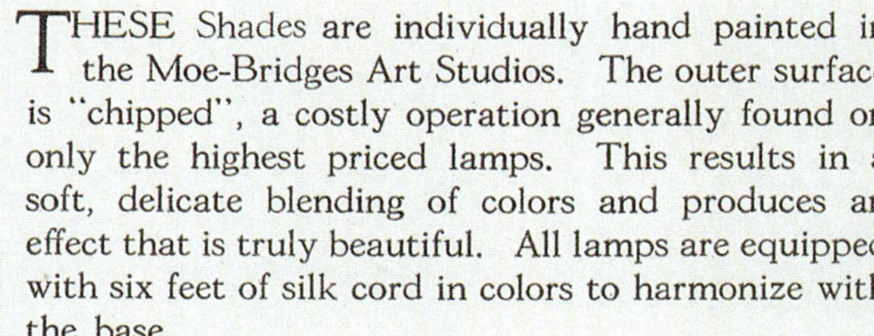

THESE Shades are individually hand painted in the Moe-Bridges Art Studios. The outer surface is "chipped", a costly operation generally found on only the highest priced lamps. This results in a soft, delicate blending of colors and produces an effect that is truly beautiful. All lamps are equipped with six feet of silk cord in colors to harmonize with the base.

B-3 — S-14
Finish, Black and Gold
Height, 13 inches
Shade, 8 inches

B-305 — S-1253
Finish, Italian Polychrome
Base, 5½ inches
Height, 15 inches
Oval Parchment Shade
With Canopy Switch

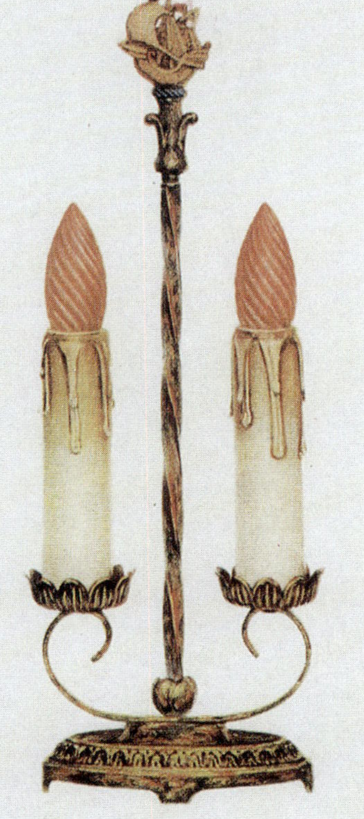

B-305
Finish, Italian Polychrome
Base, 5½ inches
Height, 15 inches
With Canopy Switch

B-304 — S-1252
Finish, Crackled Red
Base, 5½ inches
Height, 15 inches
Oval Parchment Shade
With Pull Chain

ALL Torcheres are equipped with six feet of silk cord in colors to harmonize with the finish.

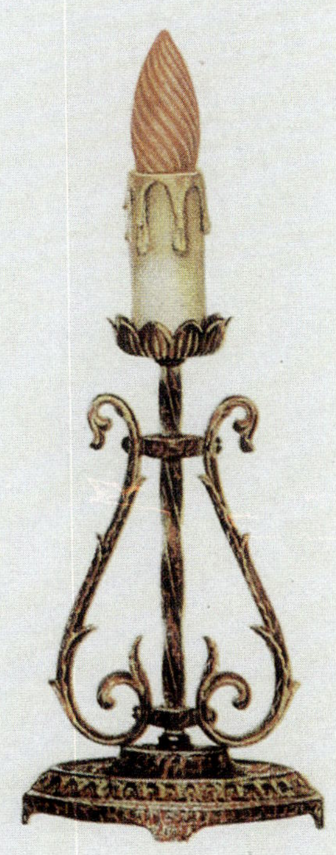

B-304
Finish, Crackled Red
Base, 5½ inches
Height, 15 inches
With Pull Chain

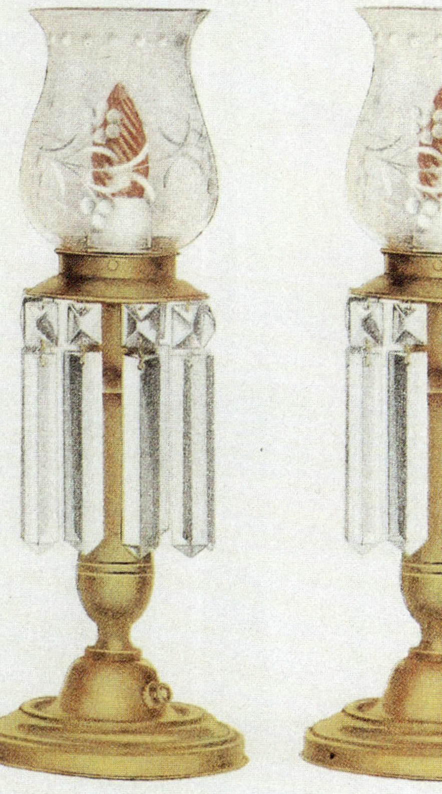

B-308
Finish, Colonial Brass
Height, 14 inches
With Canopy Switch
Astral Cut Glass Shade No. S-24218

B-306
Finish, Antique Gold
Base, 5½ inches
Height, 13½ inches
With Pull Chain

ALL Torcheres are equipped with six feet of silk cord in colors to harmonize with the finish.

B-303
Finish, Picado
Height, 18½ inches
Amber Mica Cylinder
With Pull Chain

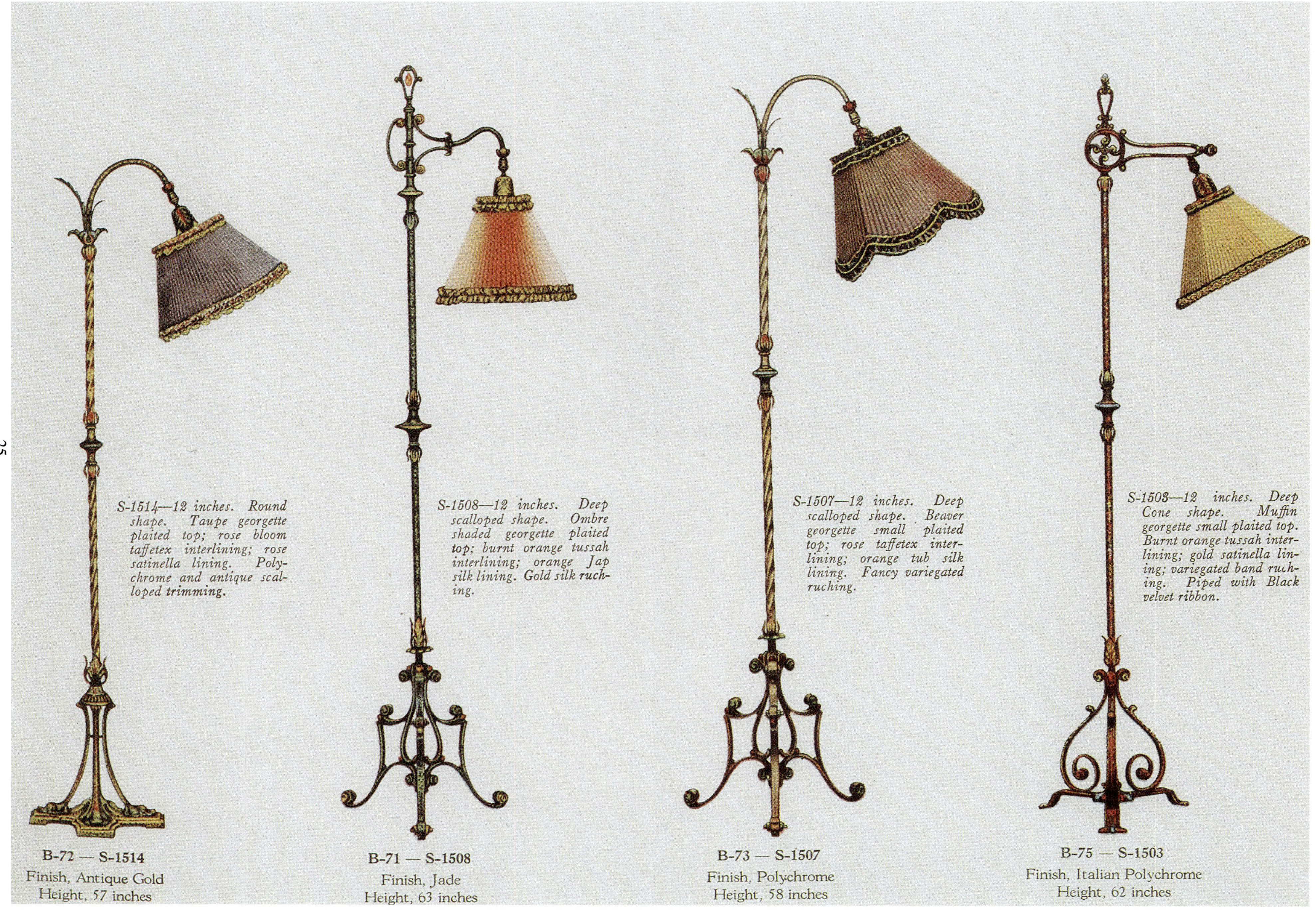

S-1514—12 inches. Round shape. Taupe georgette plaited top; rose bloom taffetex interlining; rose satinella lining. Polychrome and antique scalloped ***trimming.***

B-72 — S-1514
Finish, Antique Gold
Height, 57 inches

S-1508—12 inches. Deep scalloped shape. Ombre shaded georgette plaited ***top;*** *burnt orange tussah interlining; orange Jap silk lining. Gold silk* ***ruch****ing.*

B-71 — S-1508
Finish, Jade
Height, 63 inches

S-1507—12 inches. Deep scalloped shape. Beaver georgette small plaited top; rose taffetex interlining; orange tub silk lining. Fancy variegated ruching.

B-73 — S-1507
Finish, Polychrome
Height, 58 inches

S-1503—12 inches. Deep Cone shape. Muffin georgette small plaited top. Burnt orange tussah interlining; gold satinella lining; variegated band ruching. Piped with Black velvet ribbon.

B-75 — S-1503
Finish, Italian Polychrome
Height, 62 inches

MOE - BRIDGES LIGHTING EQUIPMENT

S-1709—16 inches. Deep oval shape. Silver and gold metallic plaited top. Gold satinella interlining; orange Jap lining. Rose and antique ruching piped with black velvet ribbon.

B-22 — S-1709
Finish, Ebony and Gold
Height, 26⅝ inches

S-1710—17 inches. Deep round bell shape. Stretched panel top of Swiss embroidered georgette. Double peach tussah interlining. Pink radium silk lining. Two-toned tan silk spray braid applied. Hand made ruching to match.

B-21 — S-1710
Finish, Crackled Red
Height, 26 inches

S-1711—16 inches. Round shape. Muffin georgette plaited top; orange interlining; gold tub silk lining. Antique and black silk braid.

B-21 — S-1711
Finish, Plaque Gold
Height, 26 inches

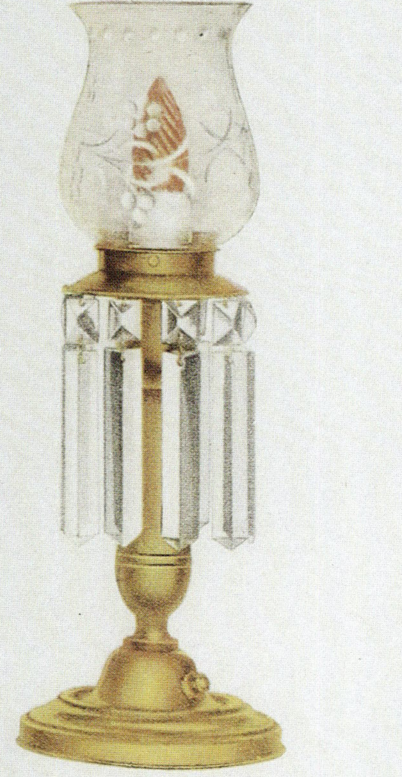
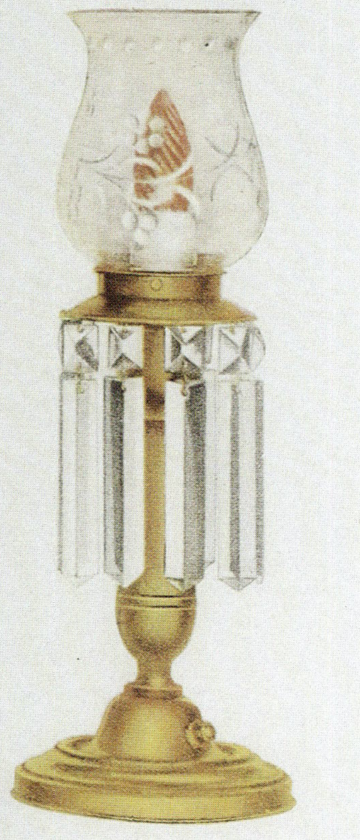
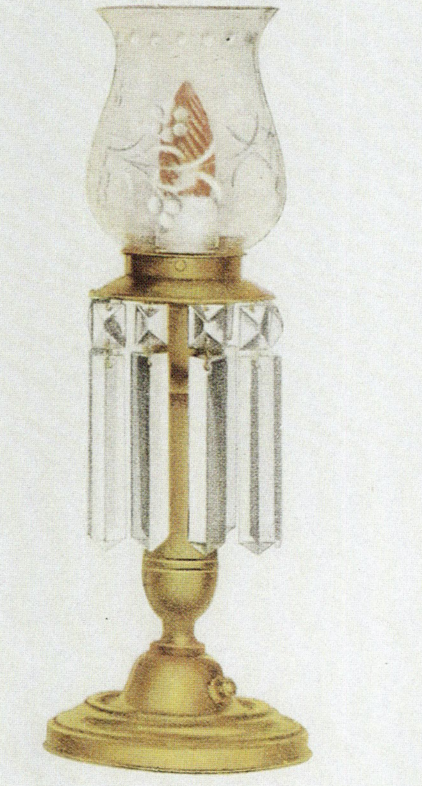
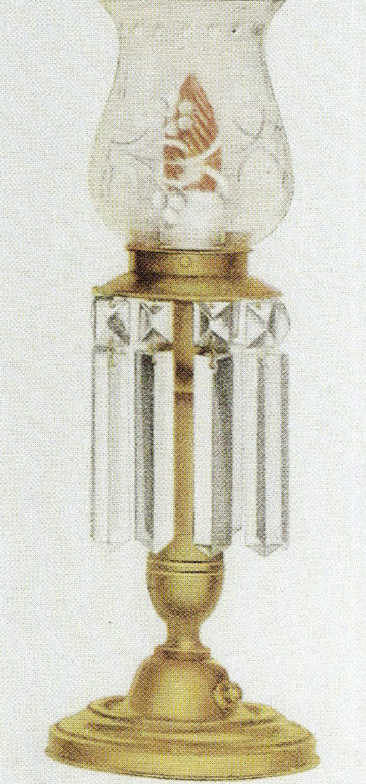

308
Early American Torchere
With Canopy Switch
Height to top of Shade, 14 inches
Diameter of Base, 5½ inches

18 S-1
Equipped with Canopy Switch
Bracket Back, 4¼ inches by 6 inches
Astral Shades — No. 24218

B-30—S-1255
(See Page 101)

422
Spread, 6½ inches
Open Bottom
Length, 30 inches

Finish:* *Colonial Brass

Finishes:* *Colonial Brass (Amber Cyl
Butler Silver (Clear Cyl

S-1710—17 inches. Deep round bell shape. Stretched panel top of Swiss embroidered georgette. Double peach tussah interlining. Pink radium silk lining. Two-toned tan silk spray braid applied. Hand made ruching to match.

B-52 — S-1710
Finish, Jade and Gold
Height, 65 inches

S-1317—16 inches. Closed top Decagon shape. Dust georgette small plaited top; peach bloom taffetex interlining; crab apple faille silk lining. Shaded green and henna gold ribbon; tan silk braid in center.

B-51 — S-1317
Finish, Jade
Height, 65 inches

S-1316 — 16 inches. Round closed top shape. Bobolink georgette small plaited top; honeydew taffetex interlining; mersham tan faille silk lining. Henna and gold shade taffeta cording and bias folds around the bottom. Four diamond squares cording and bias folds around top.

B-53 — S-1316
Finish, Polychrome
Height, 65 inches

S-1318 — 15 inches. Closed top cone shape. Cat tai georgette small plaited top, peach bloom taffetex interlining; honeydew twill silk lining. Shaded light green and peach ribbon; pastel pointed braid in center.

B-54 — S-1318
Finish, Jade and Gold
Height, 65 inches

S-1320—18 inches. Oval shape. Light bisque georgette small plaited top; peach bloom taffetex interlining; honeydew radium silk lining. Green taffeta shirred band at top and bottom finished off with light nacre shaded cord. Green and gold plaited ribbon ruching on bottom. Bead motifs applied on each side.

B-52 — S-1320
Finish, Jade and Gold
Height, 65 inches

S-1520—14 inches. Fancy deep oval band shape. Light bisque georgette small plaited top; peach bloom taffetex interlining; honeydew radium silk lining. Green taffeta shirred band at top and bottom finished off with light nacre shaded cord. Green and gold plaited ribbon ruching on bottom; bead motifs applied.

B-72 — S-1520
Finish, Jade and Gold
Height, 57 inches

S-1321—18 inches. Deep oval pointed side shape. Beige georgette small plaited top; peach bloom taffetex interlining; honeydew radium silk lining. Two rows of light and dark nacre cord. Green and gold plaited ribbon ruching at bottom. Band of flowers at top; flower trim applied on sides.

B-57 — S-1321
Finish, Italian Gold
Height, 65 inches

S-1521—14 inches. Deep oval, pointed side shape. Beige georgette plaited top; peach bloom taffetex interlining; honeydew tub silk lining. Two rows of light and dark nacre cord. Green and gold plaited ribbon ruching at bottom; band of flowers at top; flower trim applied on each side.

B-77 — S-1521
Finish, Italian Gold
Height, 56 inches

S-1323 — Imported Spring Garden Glazed Chintz. Opaque black background; natural colored Spring flowers. Gold satin taffeta ribbon binding, top and bottom. Sunproof.
B-51 — S-1323
Finish, Chinese Red
Height, 65 inches
S-1523 — Imported Spring Garden Glazed Chintz. Opaque black background; natural colored Spring flowers. Gold satin taffeta ribbon binding, top and bottom. Sunproof.
B-71 — S-1523
Finish, Chinese Red
Height, 63 inches
S-1324 — Imported Glazed Chintz. Cream background; Wild Rose design. Pink flowers, green leaves, touches of blue, lavender and yellow. Jade satin taffeta ribbon binding, top and bottom. Sunproof and Waterproof for cleaning.
B-54 — S-1324
Finish, Jade and Gold
Height, 65 inches
S-1516 — Imported Glazed Chintz. Cream background; Wild Rose design. Pink flowers, green leaves, touches of blue, lavender and yellow. Jade satin taffeta ribbon binding, top and bottom. Sunproof and Waterproof for cleaning.
B-74 — S-1516
Finish, Jade and Gold
Height, 57 inches

PORTABLE
ELECTRIC
LAMPS
CATALOGUE
NO. 20
PITTSBURGH LAMP, BRASS
AND GLASS COMPANY
PITTSBURGH, PA., U.S.A.
Pittsburgh
Pittsburgh

VERY detail in the furnishing of a room must be considered important, particularly any part of it which has to do with illumination. Every source of light is attention-compelling.

The Lamps shown in this catalogue will successfully meet the artistic as well as the practical test. Their design has been made the subject of the most careful study, with the view to the selection of patterns and color effects that will lend themselves to the most artistic schemes of interior decoration.

They are offered with full confidence that they will satisfactorily meet the demand for such service.

Pittsburgh Lamp, Brass and Glass Co.

Pittsburgh, Pa., U. S. A.

Pittsburgh

Pittsburgh

S-1325½ Electrolier Decoration A

Finished	Dimensions	
Roman Bronze with 18-inch Decoration A Shade, as shown	Total height to top of Shade,	24 in
	Extreme diameter of Round Shade,	18 in

S-1479½ Electrolier Decoration A

Finished	**Dimensions**
Roman Bronze with 14-inch Decoration A Shade, as shown	Total height to top of Shade, 22¾ in. Extreme diameter of Round Shade, 14 in.

S-1328½ Electrolier Decoration D

Finished	Dimensions	
Old Gold with 18-inch Decoration D Shade, as shown	Total height to top of Shade,	24 in.
	Extreme diameter of Round Shade,	18 in.

S-1398½ Electrolier Decoration A

Finished

Bronze Green with 18-inch Decoration A Shade, as shown

Dimensions

Total height to top of Shade,	23 in.
Extreme diameter of Round Shade,	18 in.

S-1398½ Electrolier Decoration B

Finished

Bronze Green with 18-inch Decoration B Shade, as shown

Dimensions

Total height to top of Shade, 23 in.
Extreme diameter of Round Shade, 18 in.

S-1335½C

S-1335½B

S-1335½A

S-1335½ Electrolier Decorations A, B and C

Finished

Royal Bronze with 10-inch Decoration A Shade, as shown
Balarian with 10-inch Decoration B Shade, as shown
Ivory with 10-inch Decoration C Shade, as shown

Dimensions

Total height to top of Shade, 17 in.
Extreme diameter of Round Panel Shade, 10 in.

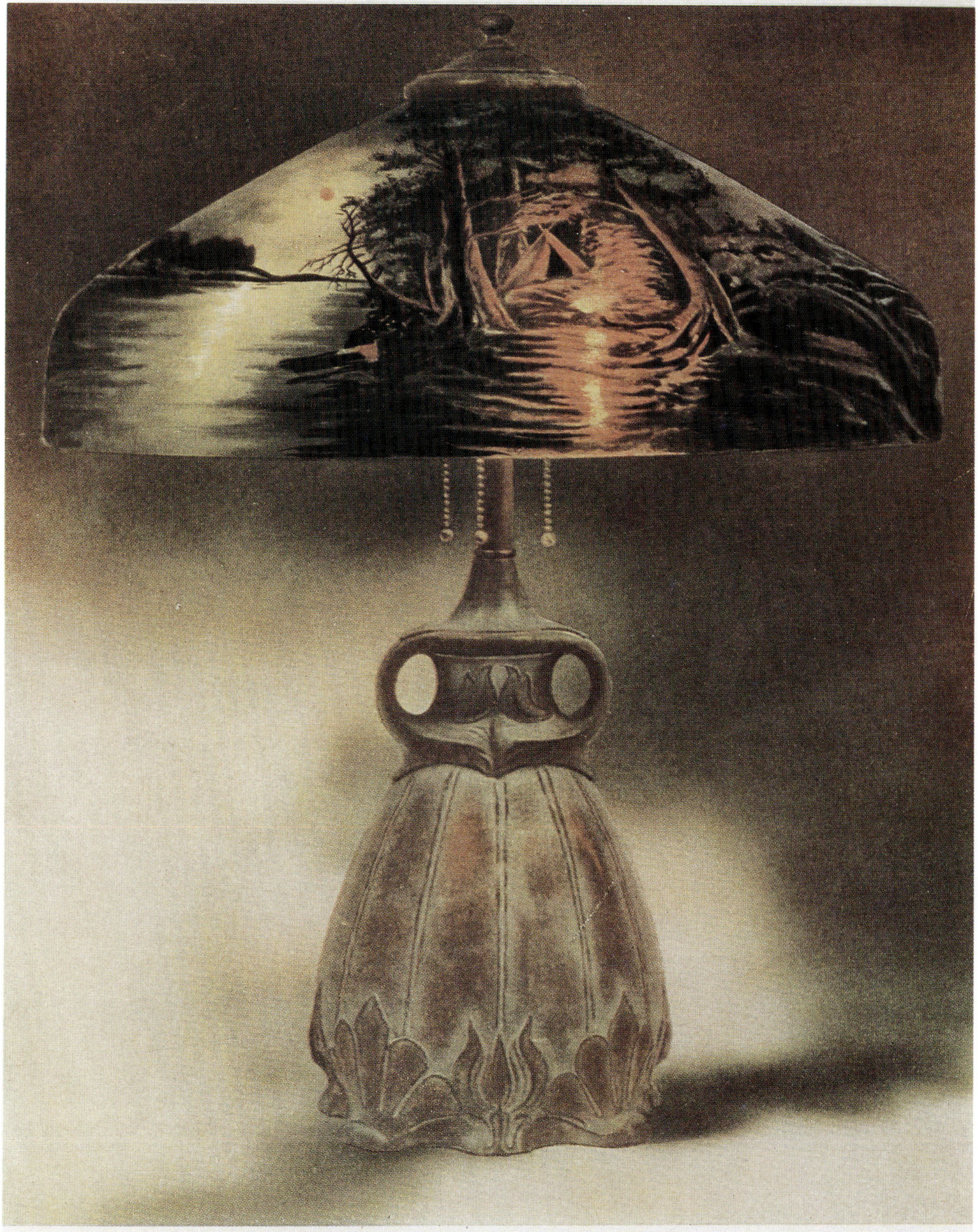

S-1398½ Electrolier Decoration C and D

Finished

Bronze Green with 18-inch Shade Decoration C, as shown, on Roughed Crystal Glass

Bronze Green with 18-inch Shade Decoration D, as shown, on Roughed Topaz Glass

Dimensions

Total height to top of Shade,	23 in.
Extreme diameter of Round Shade,	18 in.

S-1341½ Electrolier Decoration A

Finished	Dimensions	
Olive Green with 17-inch Decoration A Shade, as shown	Total height to top of Shade,	23½ in.
	Extreme diameter of Hexagon Shade,	17 in.

S-1473½ Electrolier Decoration A

Finished

Bronze Green with 18-inch Decoration A Shade, as shown, on Crystal Roughed Glass

Dimensions

Total height to top of Shade,	25 in.
Extreme diameter of Round Shade,	18 in.

S-1473½ Electrolier Decoration B

Finished

Bronze Green with 18-inch Decoration B Shade, as shown, on Topaz Roughed Glass

Dimensions

Total height to top of Shade,	25 in.
Extreme diameter of Round Shade,	18 in.

S-1473½ Electrolier Decoration C

Finished

Bronze Green with 18-inch Decoration C Shade, as shown, on Crystal Roughed Glass

Dimensions

Total height to top of Shade, 25 in.
Extreme diameter of Round Shade, 18 in.

PITTSBURGH LAMP, BRASS & GLASS COMPANY

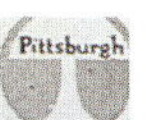

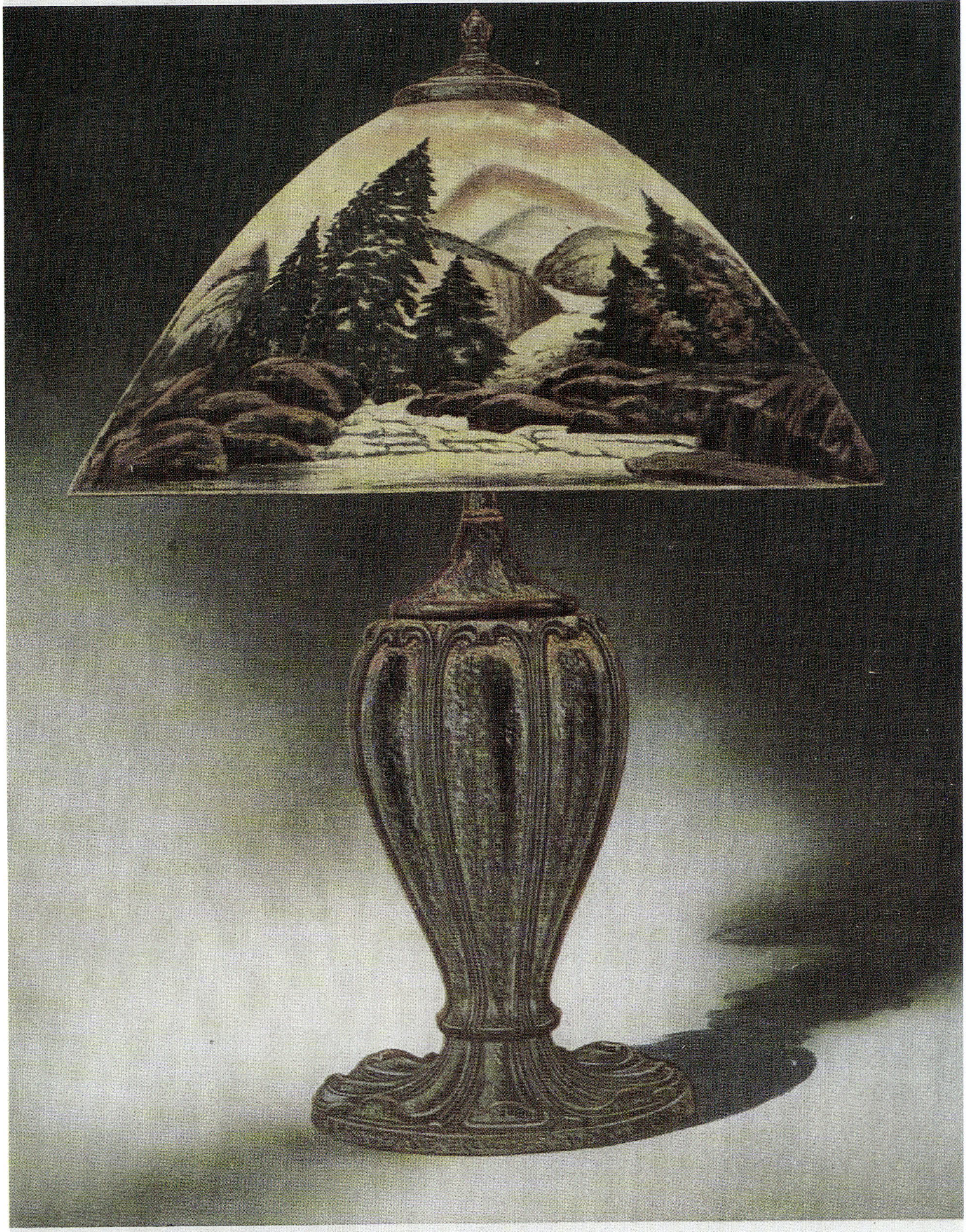

S-1473½ Electrolier Decoration D

Finished

Bronze Green with 18-inch Decoration D Shade, as shown, on Topaz Roughed Glass

Dimensions

Total height to top of Shade,	25 in.
Extreme diameter of Round Shade,	18 in.

S-1473½ Electrolier Decoration E

Finished

Bronze Green with 18-inch Decoration E Shade, as shown, on Crystal Roughed Glass

Dimensions

Total height to top of Shade, 25 in

Extreme diameter of Round Shade, 18 in

S-1473½ Electrolier Decoration F

Finished

Bronze Green with 18-inch Decoration F Shade, as shown, on Topaz Roughed Glass

Dimensions

Total height to top of Shade, 25 in.
Extreme diameter of Round Shade, 18 in.

Dec.C

Dec.B

Dec.E

Dec.F

Dec.D

Dec.A

S-1472½ Boudoir Electrolier

Finished	Diameter Shade	Total Height Portable
Old Ivory with Decoration A Shade, as shown	6½ in.	13¾ in.
Old Ivory with Decoration B Shade, as shown	6½ in.	13¾ in.
Old Ivory with Decoration C Shade, as shown	6½ in.	13¾ in.
Old Ivory with Decoration D Shade, as shown	6½ in.	13¾ in.
Roman Bronze with Decoration E Shade, as shown	6½ in.	13¾ in.
Roman Bronze with Decoration F Shade, as shown	6½ in.	13¾ in.

S-1475½ Boudoir Electrolier

Finished	Dimensions Oval Shade	Total Height Portable
Bronze Green with Decoration A Shade, as shown	9 in. x 6 in.	14½ in.
Bronze Green with Decoration B Shade, as shown	9 in. x 6 in.	14½ in.
Bronze Green with Decoration C Shade, as shown	9 in. x 6 in.	14½ in.
Bronze Green with Decoration D Shade, as shown	o in. x 6 in.	14½ in.
Bronze Green with Decoration E Shade, as shown	9 in. x 6 in.	14½ in.

S-1475½ Boudoir Electrolier

Finished	Dimensions Oval Shade	Total Height Portable
Roman Bronze with Decoration F Shade, as shown	9 in. x 6 in.	14½ in.
Roman Bronze with Decoration G Shade, as shown	9 in. x 6 in.	14½ in.
Roman Bronze with Decoration H Shade, as shown	9 in. x 6 in.	14½ in.
Roman Bronze with Decoration J Shade, as shown	9 in. x 6 in.	14½ in.
Roman Bronze with Decoration K Shade, as shown	9 in. x 6 in.	14½ in.

Boudoir Electroliers

Number	Finish Metal Parts	Glass Shade	Dimensions Shade	Total Height Portable
S-1475½	Roman Bronze	Decoration L, as shown	9 in. x 6 in.	14½ in.
S-1475½	Roman Bronze	Decoration M, as shown	9 in. x 6 in.	14½ in.
S-1476½	Bronze Green	Decoration A, as shown	7½ in. Diameter	13¾ in.
S-1476½	Bronze Green	Decoration B, as shown	7½ in. Diameter	13¾ in.
S-1476½	Yellow Ivory	Decoration C, as shown	7½ in. Diameter	13¾ in.

Boudoir Electroliers

Number	Finish Metal Parts	Total Height Portable	Diameter Shade	Description Glass Shade
S-1399½A	Bronze Green	12¾ in.	7 in.	Topaz, Scene
S-1399½B	Oxidized Silver	12¾ in.	7 in.	Delica White, Black Figures
S-1399½C	Balarian	12¾ in.	7 in.	Delica White, Rose Garland on Crystal Iced Striped
S-1399½D	Bronze Green	12¾ in.	7 in.	Delica White, "Adams" Ecru Tint Design Etching
S-1399½E	Bronze Green	12¾ in.	7 in.	Delica White, "Adams" Green Tint Design Etching
S-1399½F	Bronze Green	12¾ in.	7 in.	Delica White, "Adams" White Design Etching
S-1400½A	Ivory	12¾ in.	7 in.	Delica White, Design in Pink and Blue Tints
S-1400½B	Ivory and Green	12¾ in.	7 in.	Delica White, Design in Green Tint

PITTSBURGH LAMP, BRASS & GLASS COMPANY

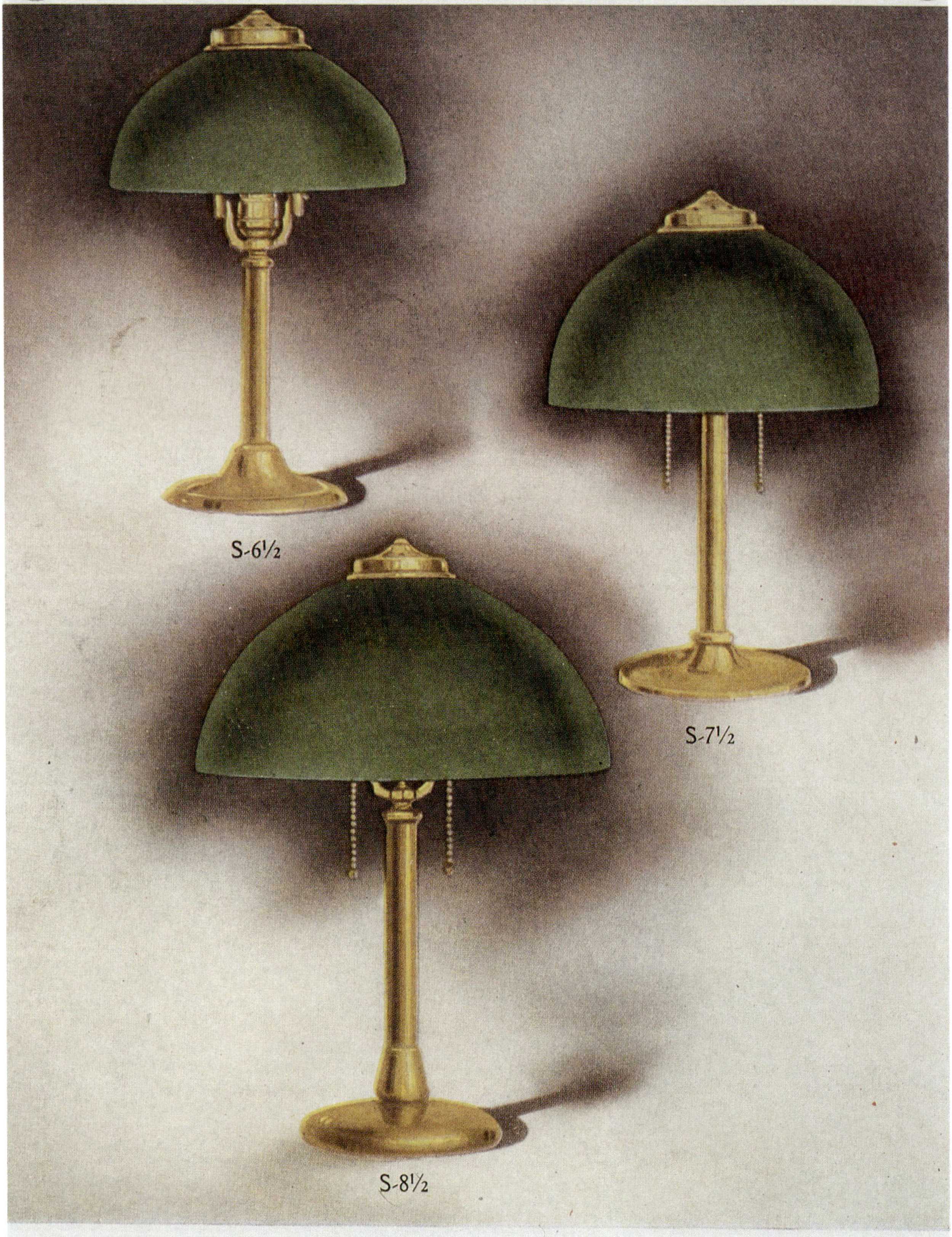
S-6½
S-7½
S-8½

University Reading Lamps

umber	Finish	Total Height	Diameter Shade	Description Glass Shade	Number Lights	Socket
-6½	Brush Brass	17 in.	10 in.	Green White Lined	1	Push
-7½	Brush Brass	19 in.	12 in.	Green White Lined	2	Pull
-8½	Brush Brass	20½ in.	14 in.	Green White Lined	2	Pull

PITTSBURGH LAMP, BRASS & GLASS COMPANY

A-1151½

A-1150½

A-1155½

A-1152½

Office and Reading Lamps

Number	Finish	Total Height	Dimensions Shade	Description Glass Shade	Number Lights
A-1150½	Brush Brass	17 in.	8¾ x 5½ in.	Green White Lined	1
A-1151½	Brush Brass	17 in.	8¾ x 5½ in.	Green White Lined	1
A-1152½	Brush Brass	17 in.	8¾ x 5½ in.	Green White Lined	1
A-1155½	Brush Brass	17 in.	8¾ x 5½ in.	Green White Lined	2

A-1428½ Electrolier Decoration A

Finished

Brush Brass and Black with Amber-Green Glass, as shown

Dimensions

Total height to top of Shade,	20	in.
Extreme diameter of Hexagon Shade,	14½	in.

PITTSBURGH LAMP, BRASS & GLASS COMPANY 

A-1429½ Electrolier Decoration A

Finished

Balarian with Amber-Green Glass, as shown

Dimensions

Total height to top of Shade, 20½ in.
Extreme diameter of Round Shade, 15½ in.

A-1430½ Electrolier Decoration A

Finished
Old Gold with Amber Glass, as shown

Dimensions
Total height to top of Shade, 21½ in.
Extreme diameter of Round Shade, 16 in.

A-1431½ Electrolier Decoration A

Finished

Polished Brass, Brown Relief with Scenic Green Glass, as shown

Dimensions

Total height to top of Shade, 22¼ in.
Extreme diameter of Round Shade, 13¾ in.

A-1401½ Electrolier Decoration A

Finished

Bronze Green with Scenic Green Glass, as shown

Dimensions

Total height to top of Shade, 21½ in.
Extreme diameter of Round Shade, 17 in.

S-1387½ Electrolier Decoration A

Finished

Brown and Silver with 14-inch Decoration A Shade, as shown

Dimensions

Total height to top of Shade, 19 in.
Extreme diameter of Round Shade, 14 in.

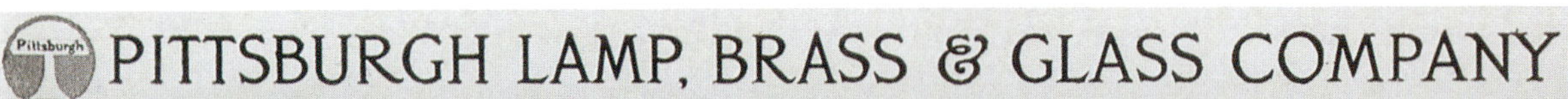

S-1397½ Electrolier Decoration A

Finished	Dimensions	
Balarian with 14-inch Decoration A Shade, as shown	Total height to top of Shade,	19 in.
	Extreme diameter of Round Shade,	14 in.

S-1397½ Electrolier Decoration B

Finished	Dimensions
Nickel and Green with 14-inch Decoration B Shade, as shown	Total height to top of Shade, 19 in.
	Extreme diameter of Round Shade, 14 in.

S-1386½ Electrolier Decoration A

Finished

Mahogany and Gold with 14-inch Decoration A Shade, as shown

Dimensions

Total height to top of Shade,	19 in.
Extreme diameter of Round Shade,	14 in.

S-1321½ Electrolier Decoration B

Finished

Pompeiian Green with 14-inch Decoration B Shade, as shown

Dimensions

Total height to top of Shade, 20¾ in.
Extreme diameter of Round Shade, 14 in.

S-1477½ Electrolier Decoration A

Finished

Green and Gold with 14-inch Decoration A Shade, as shown

Dimensions

Total height to top of Shade, 19¾ in.

Extreme diameter of Round Shade, 14 in

S-$1477\frac{1}{2}$ Electrolier Decoration B

Finished	**Dimensions**	
Brown and Gold with 14-inch Decoration B Shade, as shown	Total height to top of Shade,	$19\frac{3}{4}$ in
	Extreme diameter of Round Shade,	14 in

PITTSBURGH LAMP, BRASS & GLASS COMPANY 

S-1340$\frac{1}{2}$ Electrolier Decoration A

Finished

Ivory with 15-inch Decoration A Shade, as shown

Dimensions

Total height to top of Shade, 20 in.
Extreme diameter of Square Shade, 15 in

S-1340½ Electrolier Decoration B

Finished

Verde with 15-inch Decoration B Shade, as shown

Dimensions

Total height to top of Shade,	20 in.
Extreme diameter of Square Shade,	15 in.

S-1474½ Electrolier Decoration A

Finished

Roman Bronze with 15-inch Decoration A Shade, as shown

Dimensions

Total height to top of Shade,	19 in.
Extreme diameter of Square Shade,	15 in.

S-1474½ Electrolier Decoration B

Finished

Bronze Green with 15-inch Decoration B Shade, as shown

Dimensions

Total height to top of Shade,	19 in.
Extreme diameter of Square Shade,	15 in.

S-1390½ Electrolier Decoration A

Finished

Royal Bronze with 16-inch Decoration A Shade, as shown

Dimensions

Total height to top of Shade, 20 in.
Extreme diameter of Square Shade, 16 in.

S-1390½ Electrolier Decoration B

Finished

Balarian with 16-inch Decoration B Shade, as shown

Dimensions

Total height to top of Shade,	20 in.
Extreme diameter of Square Shade,	16 in.

S-1480½ Electrolier Decoration A

Finished

Brown and Gold with 12-inch Decoration A Shade, as shown

Dimensions

Total height to top of Shade, 19 in.
Extreme diameter of Round Shade, 12 in.

PITTSBURGH LAMP, BRASS & GLASS COMPANY

S-1480½ Electrolier Decoration D

Finished

Brown and Gold with 12-inch Decoration D Shade, as shown

Dimensions

Total height to top of Shade, 19 in.
Extreme diameter of Round Shade, 12 in.

S-1480½ Electrolier Decoration B

Finished

Brown and Gold with 12-inch Decoration B Shade, as shown

Dimensions

Total height to top of Shade,	19 in.
Extreme diameter of Round Shade,	12 in.

S-1480½ Electrolier Decoration C

Finished

Brown and Gold with 12-inch Decoration C Shade, as shown

Dimensions

Total height to top of Shade, 19 in.
Extreme diameter of Round Shade, 12 in.

PITTSBURGH LAMP, BRASS & GLASS COMPANY

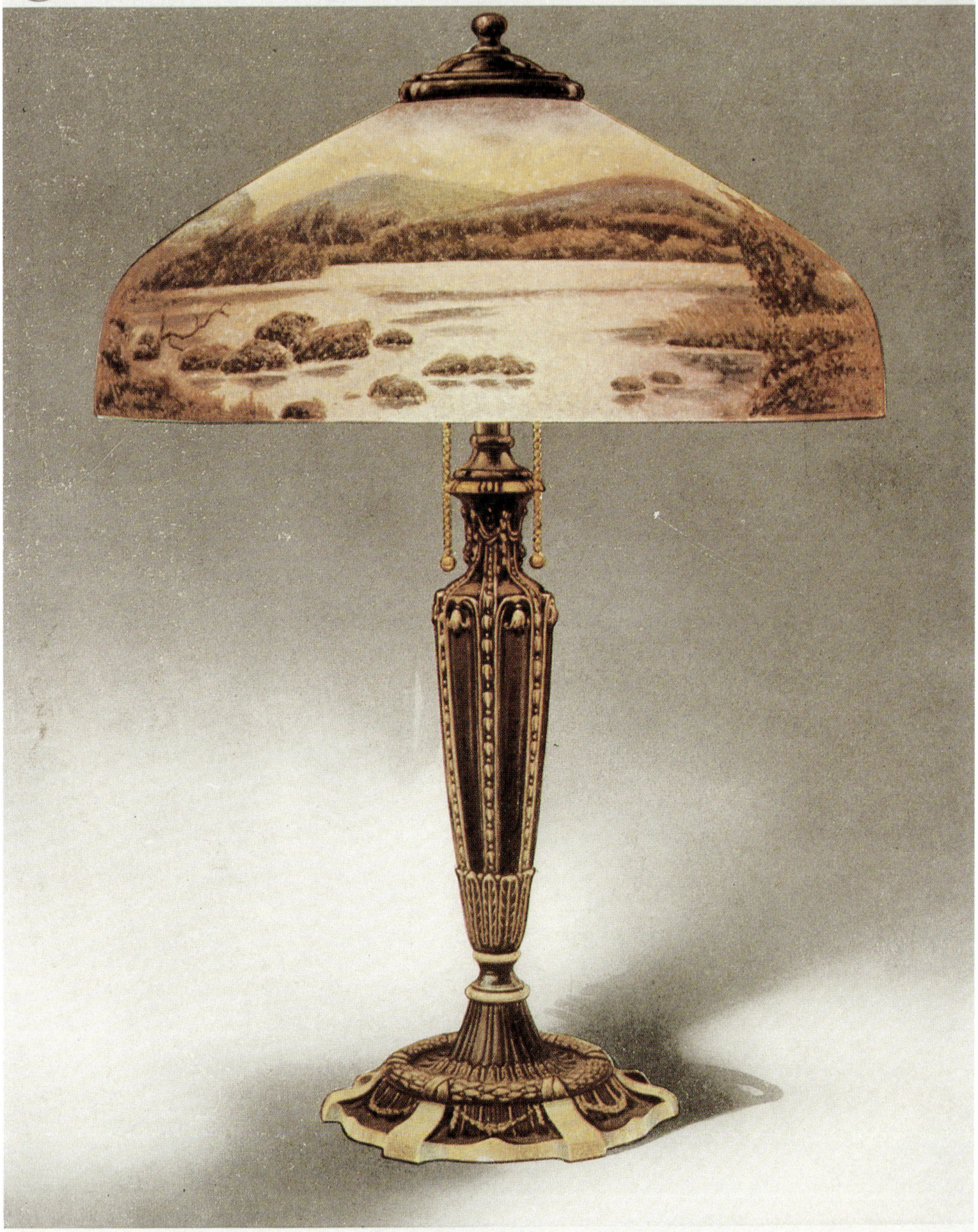

S-1324½ Electrolier Decoration F

Finished

Royal Bronze with 16-inch Decoration F Shade, as shown

Dimensions

Total height to top of Shade, 22½ in.
Extreme diameter of Round Shade, 16 in.

PITTSBURGH LAMP, BRASS & GLASS COMPANY

S-1388½ Electrolier Decoration B

Finished

Bronze Green with 16-inch Decoration B Shade, as shown

Dimensions

Total height to top of Shade, 21 in.
Extreme diameter of Round Shade, 16 in.

S-1388½ Electrolier Decoration C

Finished	Dimensions
Bronze Green with 16-inch Decoration C Shade, as shown	Total height to top of Shade, 21 in. Extreme diameter of Round Shade, 16 in.

S-1388½ Electrolier Decoration D

Finished

Flemish Brass with 16-inch Decoration D Shade, as shown

Dimensions

Total height to top of Shade, 21 in
Extreme diameter of Round Shade, 16 in

S-1478½ Electrolier Decoration A

Finished

Bronze Green with 16-inch Decoration A Shade, as shown

Dimensions

Total height to top of Shade, 21 in.
Extreme diameter of Round Shade, 16 in.

S-1478½ Electrolier Decoration B

Finished

Bronze Green with 16-inch Decoration B Shade, as shown

Dimensions

Total height to top of Shade,	21 in.
Extreme diameter of Round Shade.	16 in.

S-1478½ Electrolier Decoration C

Finished

Bronze Green with 16-inch Decoration C Shade, as shown

Dimensions

Total height to top of Shade, 21 in.
Extreme diameter of Round Shade, 16 in.

 PITTSBURGH LAMP, BRASS & GLASS COMPANY 

A-1438½ Candelabrum Decoration B

Finished

Bright Silver with Crystal Iced Glass, as shown

Dimensions

Total height to top of Shades, 17½ in.
Diameter of Round Shades, 4¾ in.
Dish, 6-inch diameter, 2½ inches deep

 PITTSBURGH LAMP, BRASS & GLASS COMPANY 

A-1438½ Candelabrum Decoration A

Finished

Gold with Amber Glass, as shown

Dimensions

Total height to top of Shades,	17½ in.
Diameter of Round Shades,	4¾ in.
Dish, 6-inch diameter, 2½ inches deep	

A-1436½ Electrolier Decoration A

Finished

Old Gold, Rose Plush Trimmings with Amber Glass, as shown

Dimensions

Total height to top of Shade, 27 in.
Extreme diameter of Round Shade, 18 in.

A-1433½ Electrolier Decoration A

Finished

Empire Gold with Amber Glass, as shown

Dimensions

Total height to top of Shade, 22¾ in.
Extreme diameter of Round Shade, 16½ in.

PITTSBURGH LAMP, BRASS & GLASS COMPANY

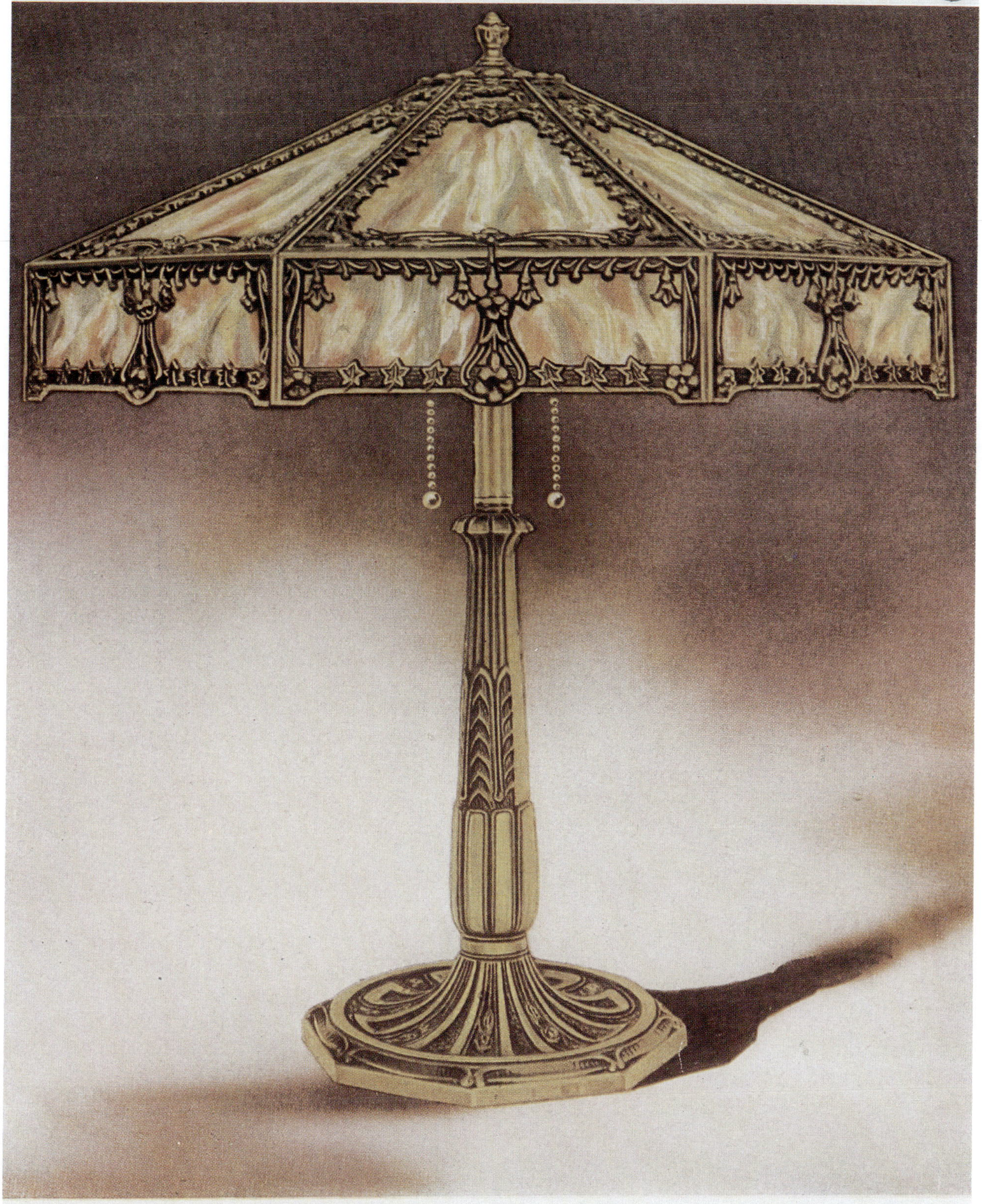

A-1432½ Electrolier Decoration A

Finished

Oxidized Brass with Amber Glass, as shown

Dimensions

Total height to top of Shade, 22½ in.
Extreme diameter of Octagon Shade, 19½ in.

PITTSBURGH LAMP, BRASS & GLASS COMPANY

A-1435$\frac{1}{2}$ Electrolier Decoration A

Finished

Bronze Green with Scenic Green Glass, as shown

Dimensions

Total height to top of Shade, 21$\frac{1}{2}$ in.
Extreme diameter of Round Shade, 18 in.

S-1350½-H

S-1351½-B

S-1351½-A

A-1343½-A

S-1355½-A

S-1353½-A

S-1352½-G

Boudoir Electroliers

Number	Finish Metal Parts	Total Height Portable	Diameter Shade	Description Glass Shade
A-1343½ A	Empire Gold	12½ in.	4¾ in.	Havana Venetian Finished
A-1343½ B	Oxidized Silver	12½ in.	4¾ in.	Crystal Venetian Finished
S-1350½ H	Balarian	13¾ in.	8 in.	Winter Scene
S-1351½ A	Ivory	13½ in.	8 in.	Delica White Garland Decoration
S-1351½ B	Ivory	13½ in.	8 in.	Delica White Rose Decoration
S-1351½ Rose	Ivory	13½ in.	8 in.	Rose Satin
S-1351½ Ecru	Ivory	13½ in.	8 in.	Ecru Satin
S-1352½ G	Balarian	13 in.	8 in.	Roses on Black Stripe
S.1353½ A	Oxidized Silver	12 in.	6 in.	Delica White Wreath Decoration
S-1353½ Rose	Oxidized Silver	12 in.	6 in.	Rose Satin
S-1353½ Ecru	Oxidized Silver	12 in.	6 in.	Ecru Satin
S-1355½ A	Ivory	12½ in.	4½ in.	Azure Satin

Lightolier Lamp Catalog
1923-24

Lightolier No. 7464.

Height, 63 in. Diameter of shade, 12 in.

Wrought iron bridge lamp, finished in polychrome. Swivelled adjustable arm and shade. Shade of finest imported parchment paper, antiqued, with closed top, and hand decorated with banded design. Depth of shade, 8 in. Key socket, 6 ft. of silk cord and two-piece plug.

Price complete.................... **$14.25**

Lightolier No. 7343.

Height, 55 in. Diameter of shade, 13 in.

Iron bridge lamp, finished in polychrome. Brass arm. Swivelled adjustable shade. Silk shade of shirred silk with silk lining and two-toned ruching, picoted. The shade can be had in choice of rose, gold, blue, mulberry or putty, with lining in contrasting color. Push button socket, 6 ft. of silk cord and two-piece plug.

Price complete.................... **$45.00**

Lightolier No. 7466.

Height, 54 in. Diameter of shade, 12 in.

Iron bridge lamp, with cast iron base finished in polychrome. Adjustable brass arm and swivelled adjustable shade. Shade of finest imported parchment paper, leather effect. Hand painted scroll design, antiqued. Push button socket, 6 ft. of silk cord, and two-piece plug.

Price complete.................... **$24.00**

Lightolier No. 7366.

Height, 63 in. Diameter of shade, 22 in.

Hand carved junior floor lamp, with fluted post, finished in polychrome. Three metal claw feet on base. Shade of beaver colored georgette, with silk lining and heavy 6 in. mulberry silk fringe. Pull chain sockets, 6 ft. of silk cord, two-piece plug and weighted base.

Price complete.................... **$80.00**

Lightolier No. 7310.

Height, 63 in. Diameter of shade, 20 in.

Solid mahogany floor lamp with fluted post. Paneled stretched silk shade in choice of rose, gold, mulberry, blue or putty, with silk lining in contrasting color, and 6 in. heavy silk fringe. Pull chain sockets, 6 ft. of silk cord, two-piece plug, and weighted base.

Price complete.................... **$53.00**

No. 7311 Same lamp finished in gold with black fluting.

No. 7312 Same lamp finished in antique ivory.

Lightolier No. 7365.

Height, 63 in. Diameter of shade, 22 in.

Junior floor lamp with fluted post, finished in gold and black. Scalloped oval shade is of shirred gold silk, with drum silk lining, and 8 in. heavy gold silk fringe. Pull chain sockets, silk cord and weighted base.

Price complete.................... **$70.00**

Lightolier No. 7453.

Height, 63 in. Diameter of shade, 22 in.
Junior floor lamp finished in antique gold and black, fluted post. Ornamental gold antique top knob. Shade of shirred silk in choice of rose, gold, mulberry, blue or putty, with silk lining in contrasting color. 6 in. heavy silk fringe. Trimmed with antique tinsel banding, and two-toned ruching, picoted, around collar. Equipped with silk pull cords, 6 ft. of silk cord, two-piece plug and weighted base.

Price complete....................**$70.00**

Lightolier No. 7452.

Height, 63 in. Diameter of shade, 21 in.
Junior floor lamp with reeded tubing in post, finished in browntone and antique gold. Octagonal shade of stretched silk in choice of rose, gold, mulberry, blue or putty, with stretched silk lining in contrasting color. 6 in. heavy silk fringe and two-toned ruching, picoted. Equipped with silk pull cords, 6 ft. of silk cord, two-piece plug and weighted base.

Price complete....................**$90.00**

Lightolier No. 7454.

Height, 63 in. Diameter of shade, 22 in.
Hand carved junior floor lamp, finished in black and gold, with ornamental antique gold top knob. Three metal claw feet on base. Oval shade of shirred silk in choice of rose, gold, mulberry, blue or putty, with silk lining in contrasting color. 6 in. heavy silk fringe, with two-toned ruching, picoted. Equipped with silk pull cords, 6 ft. of silk cord, two-piece plug and weighted base.

Price complete....................**$65.00**

"After Sunset" LIGHTOLIER

Lightolier No. 7381.

Height, 65 in. Diameter of shade, 24 in.

Floor lamp, finished in mahogany with extra heavy base. Shade is of shirred rose silk, with silk lining in same color, and 6 in. heavy rose silk fringe. Trimmed with antique gold and colored braid. Pull chain sockets, 6 ft. of silk cord, and two-piece plug.

Price complete.......................**$45.00**

No. 7382. Is the same lamp with gold shade.
No. 7383. Is the same lamp with blue shade.
No. 7384. Is the same lamp with mulberry shade.
No. 7385. Is the same lamp with putty shade.

Lightolier No. 7450.

Height, 65 in. Diameter of shade, 24 in.

Hand-carved floor lamp finished in walnut brown, with all carved parts in gold. Scalloped shade of shirred silk in choice of rose, mulberry, gold, blue or putty, with silk lining in contrasting color, and 6 in. heavy silk fringe. Trimmed with antique gold banding and two-toned ruching, picoted, around collar. Equipped with silk pull cords, 6 ft. of silk cord, two-piece plug.

Price complete.......................**$90.00**

Lightolier No. 7359.

Height, 65 in. Diameter of shade, 24 in.

Floor lamp finished in mahogany with extra heavy base. Scalloped shade is of mulberry silk, with silk lining and 6 in. heavy silk mulberry fringe. Pull chain sockets, 6 ft. of silk cord, and two-piece plug.

Price complete.......................**$55.00**

No. 7360. Is the same lamp with rose shade.
No. 7361. Is the same lamp with gold shade.
No. 7362. Is the same lamp with blue shade.

"After Sunset"
LIGHTOLIER

Lightolier No. 7347.

Height, 65 in. Diameter of shade, 24 in.

Solid mahogany floor lamp with fluted post and extra heavy base. Shade is of shirred mulberry silk, with silk lining and 6 in. heavy mulberry silk fringe. Pull chain sockets, 6 ft. of silk cord and two-piece plug.

Price complete.................... **$62.50**

No. 7348. Is the same lamp with rose shade.
No. 7349. Is the same lamp with gold shade.
No. 7350. Is the same lamp with blue shade.

Lightolier No. 7320.

Height, 65 in. Diameter of shade, 22 in.

Solid mahogany floor lamp with fluted post and extra heavy base. Shade is of stretched silk in choice of rose, gold, mulberry, blue or putty with silk lining and 8 in. heavy silk fringe. Pull chain sockets, 6 ft. of silk cord and two-piece plug.

Price complete.................... **$70.00**

Lightolier No. 7451.

Height, 67 in. Diameter of shade, 24 in.

Hand-carved floor lamp with fluted post, finished in walnut and gold leaf, antiqued. Ornamental antique gold top knob. Three metal claw feet on base. Octagonal shade of shirred silk in choice of rose, gold, mulberry, blue or putty, with drum silk lining in contrasting color, and 5 in. heavy silk fringe. Trimmed with antique gold tinsel banding. Equipped with silk pull cords, 6 ft. of silk cord, two-piece plug.

Price complete.................... **$80.00**

Lightolier No. 7489.
Height, 17½ in. Height of cylinder, 8 in.
Table torchiere finished in gold metal leaf, antiqued. Amber mica cylinder. Pull chain socket, silk cord, two-piece plug, and felt bottom.
Price, each.................................. $15.00

Lightolier No. 7493.
Height, 66 in. Height of cylinder, 8 in.
Floor torchiere, finished with gold metal leaf, antiqued. Amber mica cylinder. Pull chain socket, 6 ft. of silk cord, two-piece plug and weighted base.
Price, each........................ $35.00

Lightolier No. 7494.
Height, 16 in. Height of cylinder, 8 in.
Table torchiere finished in antique gold and polychrome. Amber mica cylinder. Candelabra base, silk cord, and felt bottom.
Price, each.................................. **$30.00**

Lightolier No. 7497.
Height, 63½ in. Diameter of lantern, 6 in.
Floor torchiere finished in antique gold and polychrome. Lantern of six panels of rough amber art glass. Pull chain socket, 6 ft. of silk cord, and two-piece plug.
Price, each......................... **$55.00**

Lightolier No. 7500.
Height, 26 in.
Diameter of shade, 20 in.
Table lamp with imported mirror blue pottery vase and ornamental antique gold knob. Cast metal base finished in antique gold. Scalloped oval shade of shirred georgette in choice of putty or blue, with silk lining and interlining. 6 in. heavy silk fringe. Trimmed with imported antique gold and colored applique. Two-toned ruching, picoted, around collar. Two-light cluster, pull chain sockets, 6 ft. of silk cord and two-piece plug.
Price complete....... **$85.00**

Lightolier No. 7499.
Height, 27 in.
Diameter of shade, 16 in.
Table lamp with imported mirror black pottery vase and ornamental antique gold knob. Cast metal base finished in antique gold. Scalloped oval shade, 10 in. deep, of plaited black georgette, with Corona gold silk lining and interlining. Trimmed with antique gold braid. Two-light cluster, pull chain sockets, 6 ft. of silk cord, and two-piece plug.
Price complete....... **$80.00**

Lightolier No. 7498.
Height, 25 in.
Diameter of shade, 20 in.
Table lamp with imported mirror blue pottery vase and ornamental antique gold knob. Cast metal base finished in antique gold. Scalloped oval shade of shirred silk in choice of blue or gold, with silk lining and 6 in. heavy silk fringe. Two-toned ruching, picoted. Two-light cluster, pull chain sockets, 6 ft. of silk cord and two-piece plug.
Price complete...................... **$65.00**

Lightolier No. 7501.
Height, 26 in.
Diameter of shade, 19 in.
Table lamp with imported mirror black pottery vase and ornamental antique gold knob. Cast metal base finished in antique gold. Circular shade of brocaded silk in choice of putty, rose, gold, blue, or peach. Silk lining and interlining. 6 in. heavy silk fringe. Trimmed with antique gold and black braid. Two-light cluster, pull chain sockets, 6 ft. of silk cord and two-piece plug.
Price complete....... **$75.00**

Lightolier No. 7502.
Height, 26 in.
Diameter of shade, 20 in.
Table lamp with imported mirror blue pottery vase and ornamental antique gold knob. Cast metal base finished in antique gold. Round shade of shirred silk in choice of gold or blue, with silk lining and 6 in. heavy silk fringe. Trimmed with antique gold and blue braid. Two-toned ruching, picoted, around collar. Two-light cluster, pull chain sockets, 6 ft. of silk cord and two-piece plug.
Price complete....... **$60.00**

Lightolier No. 7503.
Height, 27 in.
Diameter of shade, 20 in.
Table lamp with imported mirror black pottery vase and ornamental antique gold knob. Cast metal base with antique gold finish. Octagonal shade of shirred silk in choice of mulberry or gold with silk drum lining and 6 in. heavy silk fringe. Trimmed with imported antique gold applique. Two-light cluster, pull chain sockets, 6 ft. of silk cord and two-piece plug.
Price complete....................... **$70.00**

Lightolier No. 7505.
Height, 24 in.
Diameter of shade, 16 in.
Table lamp with mirror black pottery vase and ornamental antique gold knob. Empire shade, 9½ in. deep, of shirred gold silk with rose silk lining and two-toned ruching, picoted. Two-light cluster, pull chain sockets, 6 ft. of silk cord and two-piece plug.
Price complete....... **$42.00**

Lightolier No. 7504.
Height, 25 in. Diameter of shade, 18 in.
Table lamp with mirror blue pottery vase and ornamental antique gold knob. Circular shade of shirred silk in choice of blue, rose, gold or mulberry with silk lining and 6 in. heavy silk fringe. Trimmed with antique gold and blue braid. Two-light cluster, pull chain sockets, 6 ft. of silk cord and two-piece plug.
Price complete................................ **$45.00**

Lightolier No. 7495.
Height, 24 in.
Diameter of shade, 18 in.
Table lamp with mirror black pottery vase and ornamental antique gold knob. Oval shade of shirred silk in choice of gold, rose, mulberry or blue silk, with silk lining and 6 in. heavy silk fringe. Trimmed with antique gold and black braid. Two-light cluster, pull chain sockets, 6 ft. of silk cord and two-piece plug.
Price complete....... **$42.00**

Lightolier No. 7506.
Height, 24 in.
Diameter of shade, 20 in.
Table lamp with mirror black pottery vase and ornamental antique gold knob. Scalloped oval shade of shirred silk in choice of mulberry or gold, with silk drum lining and 6 in. heavy silk fringe. Trimmed with antique gold and black braid. Two-toned ruching, picoted, on collar. Two-light cluster, pull chain sockets, 6 ft. of silk cord and two-piece plug.
Price complete............................ **$48.00**

Lightolier No. 7419.
Height, 21 in. Diameter of shade, 16 in. Table lamp of Leanti metal finished in Venetian bronze. Hand decorated shade with floral design in sunset color or in green. Two pull chain sockets, 6 feet of silk cord, two-piece plug and felt bottom.
Price complete.................. **$42.00**

Lightolier No. 7308.
Height, 22 in. Diameter of shade, 16 in. Table lamp of Leanti metal, finished in bronze. Hand decorated shade in scenic design in sunset color or in green. Two pull chain sockets, 6 feet of silk cord, two-piece plug and felt bottom.
Price complete.................. **$42.00**

Lightolier No. 7328.
Height, 24 in. Diameter of shade, 18 in. Table lamp of Leanti metal, finished in dull Cyprian bronze. Hand decorated shade with scenic design in sunset color or in green. Two pull chain sockets, 6 feet of silk cord, two-piece plug and felt bottom.
Price complete.................. **$50.00**

Lightolier No. 7478.
Height, 21 in. Diameter of shade, 16 in.
Table lamp finished in Fresco gold. Shade of six panels of amber art glass set in frame. Two pull chain sockets, 6 feet of silk cord, two-piece plug and felt bottom.
Price complete.................. $22.00

Lightolier No. 7335.
Height, 24 in. Diameter of shade, 19 in.
Table lamp finished in Egyptian bronze. Shade of eight panels of amber art glass, set in frame. Two pull chain sockets, 6 feet of silk cord, two-piece plug and felt bottom.
Price complete.................. $27.00

Lightolier No. 7334.
Height, 15 in. Diameter of shade, 8 in.
Boudoir lamp, finished in antique ivory and polychrome. Shade of four panels of amber art glass set in frame. Push button socket, 6 feet of silk cord, two-piece plug and felt bottom.
Price complete.................. $12.00

Lightolier No. 7477.
Height, 24½ in. Diameter of shade, 19 in.
Table lamp, finished in silver gray with copper highlights. Shade of eight panels of amber art glass set in frame. Two pull chain sockets, six feet of silk cord, two-piece plug and felt bottom.
Price complete.................. $33.00

Lightolier No. 7363.

Height, 26 in. Diameter of shade, 20 in.
Table lamp finished in gold and polychrome, antiqued. Scalloped oval shade of Copenhagen blue with drum silk lining and 8 in. heavy blue silk fringe. Two-toned ruching, picoted. Two pull chain sockets, 6 feet of silk cord, and two-piece plug.

Price complete..................... **$65.00**

Lightolier No. 7330.

Height, 22½ in. Diameter of shade, 14 in.

Table lamp, finished in gold and polychrome, antiqued. Shade of shirred silk in choice of rose, gold, blue, mulberry or putty, with drum silk lining in contrasting color, and 5 in. heavy silk fringe, with four silk tassels, and two-toned ruching, picoted. One push-button socket, 6 feet of silk cord, and two-piece plug.

Price complete.. **$35.00**

Lightolier No. 7447.

Height, 19 in Diameter of shade, 10 in.
Boudoir lamp, finished in French gray and polychrome. Shade of shirred putty colored silk with rose silk lining, and overlay of lace. Trimmed with antique gold braid and antique gold drops. Push button socket, 6 ft. of silk cord, two-piece plug, and felt bottom.

Price complete.................... **$35.00**

Lightolier No. 7448.

Height, 17 in. Diameter of shade, 10 in.
Boudoir lamp, finished in antique gold and polychrome. Scalloped shade of shirred chiffon in choice of rose, gold, mulberry, blue or putty, lined and interlined with silk. Trimmed with antique gold braid. Push button socket, 6 ft. of silk cord, two-piece plug and felt bottom.

Price complete.................... **$21.50**

Lightolier No. 7496.

Height, 19 in. Diameter of shade, 10 in.
Boudoir lamp, finished in Roman gold and polychrome. Round shade of shirred georgette in choice of rose, gold, mulberry or blue, with skirt of plaited georgette. Push button socket, 6 ft. of silk cord, two-piece plug and felt bottom.

Price complete.................... **$30.00**

Lightolier No. 7474.

Height, 14½ in. Diameter of shade, 10½ in.
Boudoir lamp, imported decorated pottery vase, gold plated metal base. Lamp in choice of blue and lilac, lilac and lavender, blue and green or lavender and rose. Oval shirred taffeta shade in choice of rose, gold, blue or mulberry. Silk lining and antique silver braid. Trimmed with hand-made rosebuds. Push button socket, silk cord, two-piece plug and felt bottom.

Price complete.................... **$25.00**

Lightolier No. 7449.

Height, 18 in.
Candlestick finished in antique silver and polychrome. Candle socket, 6 feet of silk cord, two-piece plug and felt bottom.

Price complete.................... **$15.00**

Lightolier No. 7518 is the same lamp finished in antique gold and polychrome.

Lightolier No. 7473.

Height, 14 in. Diameter of shade, 10 in.
Boudoir lamp made of Leanti metal, finished in Roman gold. Scalloped oval shade of shirred silk in choice of rose, gold, mulberry, blue or putty, with silk lining in same color. Trimmed with antique gold braid. Push button socket, 6 feet of silk cord, two-piece plug and felt bottom.

Price complete.................... **$15.00**

Lightolier No. 7516 is the same lamp finished in ivory.
Lightolier No. 7517 is the same lamp finished in verde green.

Lightolier No. 7468.
Height, 14 in.
Diameter of shade, 8 in.
Boudoir lamp in ivory finish with hand-painted floral decoration and blue banding. Scalloped shade of shirred rose silk, with rose silk lining. Three flower buds on shade. Push button socket, 6 ft. of silk cord, two-piece plug and felt bottom.
Price complete. . . **$10.00**

Lightolier No. 7469.
Height, 14 in.
Diameter of shade, 8 in.
Mahogany boudoir lamp finished with hand-painted floral decorations and blue banding. Round shade of shirred blue silk, with blue silk lining. Four flower buds on shade. Push button socket, 6 ft. of silk cord, two-piece plug and felt bottom.
Price complete. . . **$10.00**

Lightolier No. 7467.
Height, 14 in. Diameter of shade, 8 in.
Boudoir lamp in ivory finish with hand painted floral decoration, and blue colored banding. Octagonal shade of shirred mulberry silk with mulberry silk lining. Four flower buds on shade. Push button socket, 6 ft. of silk cord, two-piece plug and felt bottom.
Price complete. **$10.00**

Lightolier No. 7472.
Height, 14 in.
Diameter of shade, 8 in.
Boudoir lamp in ivory finish, with hand-painted floral decoration and rose-colored banding. Shade of finest imported parchment, leather effect, with hand-painted floral decoration. Push button socket, 6 ft. of silk cord, two-piece plug and felt bottom.
Price complete. . . **$10.00**

Lightolier No. 7470.
Height, 14 in.
Diameter of shade, 8 in.
Mahogany boudoir lamp finished with hand-painted floral decoration. Shade of finest imported parchment, leather effect, with hand-painted floral decoration. Push button socket, 6 ft. of silk cord, two-piece plug and felt bottom.
Price complete. . . **$10.00**

Lightolier No. 7471.
Height, 14 in.
Diameter of shade, 8 in.
Mahogany boudoir lamp, finished with hand-painted floral decoration and violet colored banding. Shade of finest imported parchment, leather effect, with hand-painted floral decoration. Push button socket, 6 ft. of silk cord, two-piece plug and felt bottom.
Price complete. . . **$10.00**

Lightolier No. 7316.

Height, 15 in.

Diameter of shade, 7 in.

Boudoir lamp, made of Leanti metal, finished in Antique Ivory. Hand-decorated glass shade with floral design. Push button socket, 6 ft. of silk cord, two-piece plug and felt bottom.

Price complete...**$13.00**

Lightolier No. 7315.

Height, 15 in.

Diameter of shade, 7 in.

Boudoir lamp, made of Leanti metal, finished in Roman gold. Hand-decorated glass shade with floral design. Push button socket, 6 ft. of silk cord, two-piece plug and felt bottom.

Price complete...**$13.00**

Lightolier No. 7314.

Height, 15 in. Diameter of shade, 7 in.

Boudoir lamp, made of Leanti metal, finished in myrtle green. Hand-decorated glass shade in scenic design. Push button socket, 6 ft. of silk cord, two-piece plug and felt bottom.

Price complete......**$13.00**

Lightolier No. 7388.

Height, 15 in.

Diameter of shade, 7 in.

Boudoir lamp, made of Leanti metal, finished in myrtle green. Hand-decorated glass shade in scenic design. Push button socket, 6 ft. of silk cord, two-piece plug and felt bottom.

Price complete...**$13.00**

Lightolier No. 7389.

Height, 15 in.

Diameter of shade, 7 in.

Boudoir lamp, made of Leanti metal, finished in Roman gold. Hand-decorated glass shade. Push button socket, 6 ft. of silk cord, two-piece plug and felt bottom.

Price complete...**$13.00**

Lightolier No. 7387.

Height, 15 in.

Diameter of shade, 7 in.

Boudoir lamp, made of Leanti metal, finished in Antique Ivory. Hand-decorated glass shade in floral design. Push button socket, 6 ft. of silk cord, two-piece plug and felt bottom.

Price complete...**$13.00**

Lightolier No. 7404.

Height, 4 in. Width of shield, 4 in.

Candle shield of shirred gold silk with drum lining of rose silk. Black moss edging. Shield can also be had in the following combinations of colors: Rose lined rose with black moss, blue lined blue with blue moss.

Price.......................................**$3.00**

Lightolier No. 7403.

Height, 4 in. Width of shield, 4 in.

Candle shield of shirred gold silk with drum lining of rose silk. Braid of antique gold. Shield can also be had in the following combinations of colors: Rose lined rose, blue lined rose.

Price......................................**$2.50**

Lightolier No. 7405.

Height, 4 in. Diameter of shade, 4 in.

Candle shade of shirred gold silk, lined with rose silk and with black moss trimming. This shade can also be had in the following combinations of colors: Rose lined rose with black moss, blue lined rose with blue moss, tan lined rose with orchid moss.

Price...............................**$2.80**

Lightolier No. 7402.

Height, 4 in. Diameter of shade, 4 in.

Candle shade of shirred blue silk with rose silk lining. Braid trimming of antique gold with four flower buds. Shade can also be had in the following combinations of colors: Gold lined rose, tan lined rose, and rose lined rose.

Price....................................**$3.00**

Lightolier No. 7407.

Height, 4 in. Diameter of shade, 4 in.

Candle shade of shirred rose silk with rose silk lining. Antique gold braid trimming. Shade can also be had in the following combinations of colors: Gold lined rose, blue lined rose.

Price...............................**$1.75**

Lightolier No. 7484.

Height, 4 in. Width of shield, 4 in.

Candle shield of finest imported parchment paper, leather effect, antiqued. Hand painted with red striping.

Price...............................**$2.00**

Lightolier No. 7485.

Height, 4 in. Width of shield, 4 in.

Candle shield of finest imported parchment paper, leather effect, antiqued. Hand painted with floral decoration and rose striping.

Price...............................**$2.40**

Lightolier No. 7411.

Height, 4 in. Width of shield, 4 in.

Candle shield of finest imported parchment paper, leather effect, antiqued. Hand painted with fruit and floral decoration.

Price...............................**$2.00**

Lightolier No. 7481.

Height, 4 in. Diameter of shade, 4 in. Candle shade of finest imported parchment paper, leather effect, antiqued. Hand painted with red striping.

Price...............**$1.75**

Lightolier No. 7480.

Height, 4 in. Diameter of shade, 4 in. Candle shade of finest imported parchment paper, leather effect, antiqued. Hand painted with floral decoration and rose striping.

Price...............**$2.25**

Lightolier No. 7479.

Height, 4 in. Diameter of shade, 4 in. Candle shade of finest imported parchment paper, leather effect, antiqued. Hand painted with armorial decoration.

Price...............**$2.25**

Lightolier No. 7427.

Height, 4 in. Diameter of shade, 4 in. Candle shade of finest imported parchment paper, leather effect, antiqued. Hand painted with fruit and floral decoration.

Price...............**$2.00**

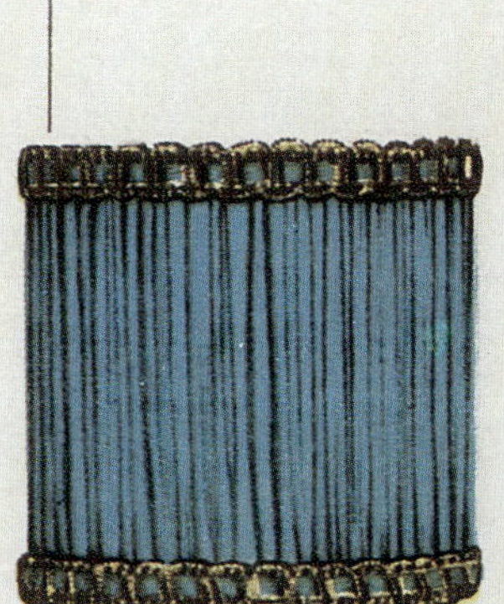

Lightolier No. 7491.
Height, 4 in. Width of shield, 4 in.
Candle shield of shirred blue silk with rose silk lining and trimmed with antique gold and blue braid. Shield can also be had in the following combinations of colors: Rose lined rose, gold lined rose, tan lined rose.
Price.............................. **$2.75**

Lightolier No. 7492.
Height, 5¼ in. Width, 10½ in.
Two-light candle bracket screen with adjustable holders to fit size of bracket, made of shirred blue silk with rose silk lining and antique gold and blue braid. Screen can also be had in the following combinations of colors: Rose lined rose, gold lined rose, tan lined rose.
Price.............................. **$7.50**

Lightolier No. 7490.
Height, 4 in. Diameter of shade, 4 in.
Candle shade of shirred blue silk, lined with rose silk and trimmed with antique gold and blue braid. This shade can also be had in the following combinations of colors: Rose lined rose, gold lined rose, tan lined rose.
Price.............................. **$2.40**

Lightolier No. 7483.
Height, 6 in. Width of shield, 4 in.
Candle shield of finest imported parchment paper, leather effect. Hand painted with armorial design and blue banding.
Price.............................. **$2.75**

Lightolier No. 7487.
Height, 5¼ in. Width, 10½ in.
Two-light candle bracket screen, with adjustable holders to fit size of bracket. Made of finest imported parchment paper, leather effect, antiqued. Hand painted with armorial design.
Price.............................. **$6.25**

Lightolier No. 7482.
Height, 4½ in. Diameter of shade, 5 in.
Fixture shade with 2¼ in. holder, made of finest imported parchment paper, leather effect, antiqued. Hand painted with armorial design.
Price.............................. **$3.00**

Lightolier No. 7486.
Height, 5¼ in. Width, 10½ in.
Two-light candle bracket screen, with adjustable holders to fit size of bracket. Made of finest imported parchment paper, leather effect, antiqued. Hand painted with floral design and rose striping.
Price.............................. **$5.75**

Lightolier No. 7488.
Height, 5¼ in. Width, 10½ in.
Two-light candle bracket screen, with adjustable holders to fit size of bracket. Made of finest imported parchment paper, leather effect, antiqued. Hand painted with figured design.
Price.............................. **$5.75**

"After Sunset"
LIGHTOLIER

Lightolier No. 7476.
Height, 14 in.
Boudoir doll, waxed head, natural gray wig. Trimmed with taffeta dress in choice of Copenhagen blue, rose, or orchid, with braid. Porcelain socket, silk cord and two-piece plug.
Price complete...............**$7.00**

Lightolier No. 7475.
Height, 16 in.
Boudoir doll, waxed head, natural blonde wig. Trimmed with taffeta dress in choice of rose, Copenhagen blue or orchid, and antique gold and colored braid. Porcelain socket, silk cord, two-piece plug.
Price complete...............**$9.00**

Lightolier No. 7313.
Height to swivel, 7 in. Diameter of base, 5 in. Desk lamp, made of Leanti metal, finished in bronze or myrtle green. Swivelled adjustable shade. Push button socket, 6 ft. of silk cord, two-piece plug and felt bottom.
Price complete.... ....**$9.00**

Lightolier No. 4001.
Height to arm, 38 in. Flexolier arm, 21 in. Diameter of base, 9 in.
Flexible smoking stand finished in Lightolier bronze or myrtle green. Flexible arm, metal shade, finished inside in aluminum. Push button socket, 8 feet of silk cord, two-piece plug and felt bottom.
Price complete.....................**$19.00**

Lightolier No. 3890.
Height of arm, extended, 15 in.
Flexible reading lamp, finished in Lightolier bronze. Flexible stem, metal shade, finished inside in aluminum. Push button socket, 6 ft. of silk cord, two-piece plug and felt bottom.
Price complete.......................**$8.00**

"After Sunset" LIGHTOLIER

Lightolier No. 7465.

Height, 63 in. Diameter of shade, 12 in.

Wrought iron bridge lamp, finished in polychrome. Hand hammered leaf work on legs. Swivelled adjustable arm and shade. Scalloped shade of finest imported parchment paper, leather effect, hand decorated with floral design. Key socket, 6 ft. of silk cord, and two-piece plug.

Price complete.................... **$30.00**

Lightolier No. 7463.

Height, 60 in. Diameter of shade, 14 in.

Wrought iron bridge lamp, finished in antique iron. Swivelled adjustable arm and shade. Shade of finest imported parchment paper, leather effect, and decorated with scroll design. Push button socket, 6 ft. of silk cord and two-piece plug.

Price complete.................... **$40.00**

Lightolier No. 7462.

Height, 64 in. Diameter of shade, 12 in.

Wrought iron bridge lamp, finished in antique iron. Adjustable arm and swivelled adjustable shade. Shade of finest imported parchment paper, leather effect, with hand painted scroll design. Push button socket, 6 ft. of silk cord and two-piece plug.

Price complete.................... **$36.00**

"After Sunset"
LIGHTOLIER

Lightolier No. 7457.

Height, 55 in. Diameter of shade, 12 in.

Bridge lamp, finished in antique gold, and black, fluted post. Swivelled adjustable shade. Shade of shirred silk, in choice of rose, gold, mulberry, blue or putty, with silk lining in contrasting color. 4 in. heavy silk fringe and two-toned ruching, picoted. Push button socket, 6 ft. of silk cord, two-piece plug and weighted base.

Price complete.....................**$55.00**

Lightolier No. 7459.

Height, 55 in. Diameter of shade, 13 in.

Bridge lamp with fluted post, finished in antique gold and polychrome. Swivelled adjustable shade, shirred silk shade in choice of rose, gold, mulberry, blue or putty, with silk lining in contrasting color, two-toned ruching, picoted. Push button socket, 6 ft. of silk cord, two-piece plug and weighted base.

Price complete.....................**$47.50**

Lightolier No. 7455.

Height, 55 in. Diameter of shade, 12 in.

Hand-carved bridge lamp with fluted post finished in browntone and stippled antique burnished gold. Three metal claw feet on base. Swivelled adjustable shade. Shirred silk shade in choice of rose, gold, mulberry, blue or putty, with silk lining in contrasting color. 5 in. heavy silk fringe. Trimmed with plaited ruffle with black velvet band. Push button socket. 6 ft. of silk cord, two-piece plug and weighted base.

Price complete.....................**$60.00**

"After Sunset" LIGHTOLIER

Lightolier No. 7461.

Height, 55 in. Diameter of shade, 12 in.

Bridge lamp with reeded tubing in post, finished in black and gold. Swivelled adjustable shade. Shade of shirred silk in choice of rose, gold, mulberry, blue or putty, with silk lining in contrasting color. 5 in. heavy silk fringe with four tassels and two-toned ruching, picoted. Push button socket, 6 ft. of silk cord, two-piece plug and weighted base.

Price complete........................**$51.00**

Lightolier No. 7456.

Height, 55 in. Diameter of shade, 13 in.

Hand carved bridge lamp, finished in black and gold. Three metal claw feet on base. Scalloped oval shade of shirred silk, in choice of rose, gold, mulberry, blue or putty, and lined with silk in a contrasting color. 5 in. heavy silk fringe. Push button socket, 6 ft. of silk cord, two-piece plug and weighted base.

Price complete........................**$55.00**

Lightolier No. 7460.

Height, 55 in. Diameter of shade, 12 in.

Bridge lamp, finished in browntone and stippled antique gold. Fluted post, swivelled adjustable shade. Georgette shade in choice of rose, gold, mulberry, blue or putty, with two-toned ruching, picoted. Pull chain socket, 6 ft. of silk cord, two-piece plug and weighted base.

Price complete........................**$48.00**

"After Sunset"
LIGHTOLIER
Lightolier No. 7337.
Height, 55 in. Diameter of shade, 12 in.
Hand carved bridge lamp with fluted post, finished in polychrome and gold. Three metal claw feet on base. Swivelled adjustable shade. Shade is of shirred gold silk, with silk lining and 5 in. heavy gold silk fringe. Push button socket, 6 ft. of silk cord, two-piece plug and weighted base.
Price complete.......................$56.00
Lightolier No. 7458.
Height, 55 in. Diameter of shade, 13 in.
Hand carved bridge lamp, finished in walnut and antique gold leaf. Three metal claw feet on base. Swivelled adjustable shade. Shade of stretched silk in choice of rose, gold, mulberry, blue or putty, with drum silk lining in contrasting color, and 4 in. heavy silk fringe. Trimmed with silk tinsel braid, and two-toned ruching, picoted, around collar. Push button socket, 6 ft. of silk cord, two-piece plug and weighted base.
Price complete.......................$80.00
Lightolier No. 7378.
Height, 55 in. Diameter of shade, 11 in.
Solid mahogany bridge lamp, with fluted post. Swivelled adjustable shade in choice of rose, gold, mulberry, blue or putty, with silk lining. Two-toned ruching, picoted. Push button socket, 6 ft. of silk cord, two-piece plug and weighted base.
Price complete.......................$35.00
Lightolier No. 7379 is the same lamp in gold finish.
Lightolier No. 7380 is the same lamp in ivory finish.

"ALADDIN"

Electric Portable

LAMPS

DISTRIBUTED BY

COMMERCIAL ELECTRICAL SUPPLY CO.

DIVISION OF

WESTINGHOUSE ELECTRIC SUPPLY COMPANY

320 S. Broadway
St. Louis, Mo.

366 Madison,
Memphis, Tenn.

ALADDIN MANUFACTURING CO.

MUNCIE, INDIANA, U. S. A.

"ALADDIN" PIANO AND RADIO LAMPS

STANDARD PACKAGE—ANY SIX

No. 108/503
POMPEIAN BRONZE
LIST, $8.50 EACH

Shades Nos. 501, No. 502, and No. 503 are Hand-Painted Glass, Length, 8½".
LIST, Shade Only, **$2.50** EACH.

Stands Only, Adjustable, 10".
LIST, Shade Only, **$6.00** EACH.

No. 109/502
VERDE GREEN
LIST, $8.50 EACH

No. 110/501
ANTIQUE GOLD
LIST, $8.50 EACH

All "ALADDIN" Piano and Radio Lamps Packed in Individual Cartons.

"ALADDIN" ALL METAL PIANO LAMP

THE PERFECT PIANO LAMP

No Tools Required

Takes But a Second to Attach

Held firmly in place by specially constructed Spring.

Padded with Felt to protect Front of Piano.

LIST,
$4.00
EACH

Packed one to a Carton

Standard Package, 12

No. 1965	Grained Mahogany
No. 1967	Grained Walnut
No. 1968	Statuary Bronze

[Please order by number]

The Perfect Piano Lamp

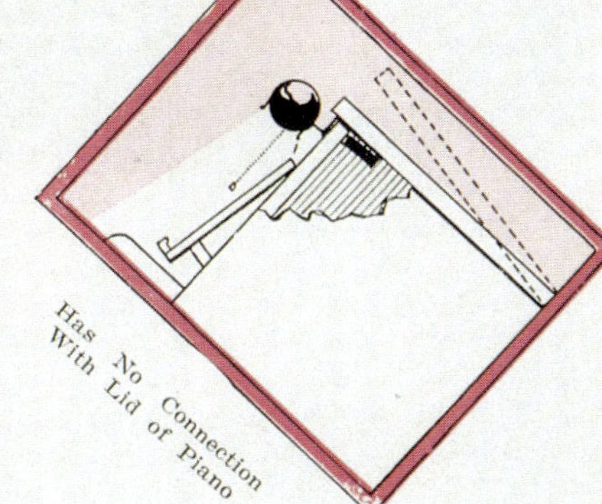

Has No Connection With Lid of Piano

MODIFIED MODERNISTIC TWO-LIGHT CANDLE FLOOR LAMPS WITH BRIDGE TO MATCH

STANDARD PACKAGE—ANY FOUR

Shades No. 2751 and **No.** 2851, at the left, are Gold Tinted Alanoid, Laced.

No. 2352/2751 COMPLETE, LIST, $22.50

No. 2352
Swedish Iron **Plated** Stand
Height of Stand, 63″
LIST, Stand Only,
$15.00 EACH

No. 2751
Shade
Size 10x15x20″
LIST, Shade Only,
$7.50 EACH

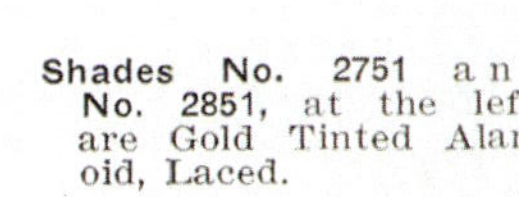

No. 1493/2851 COMPLETE, LIST, $17.50

No. 1493
Swedish Iron Stand
Height of Stand, 61″
LIST, Stand Only,
$12.50 EACH

No. 2851
Shade
Size 8x9x13″
LIST, Shade Only,
$5.00 EACH

No. 2351/1762 COMPLETE, LIST, $24.50

No. 2351
Antique Gold **Plated** Stand
Height of Stand, 64″
LIST, Stand Only,
$16.00 EACH

No. 1762
Shade
Size 10x15x20″
LIST, Shade Only,
$8.50 EACH

No. 1488/1850 COMPLETE, LIST, $18.50

No. 1488
Antique Gold **Plated** Stand
Height of Stand, 61″
LIST, Stand Only,
$13.50 EACH

No. 1850
Shade
Size 8x9x13″
LIST, Shade Only,
$5.00 EACH

Shades No. 1762 and **No.** 1850, at the right, are Varigated Alanoid with Green and Red predominating.

FLOOR AND BRIDGE LAMPS TO MATCH

STANDARD PACKAGE—ANY FOUR

No. 1397/2357 COMPLETE, LIST, $13.50

No. 1397 Antique Gold **Plated** Stand Only, Height of Stand 61″.
LIST, $8.50 EACH

No. 2357 **Shade** Only, Size 11 x 17″,
LIST, $5.00 EACH

No. 1497/2457 COMPLETE, LIST, $12.00

No. 1497 Antique Gold-**Plated** Bronze Stand only,
Height of Stand, 58″.
LIST, $8.50 EACH

No. 2457 **Shade** Only, Size 8 x 11″,
LIST, $3.50 EACH

Shades are Leatherette Parchment with Modernistic Designs, Antique Finish, Laced.

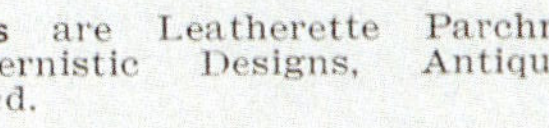

No. 1398/2356 COMPLETE, LIST, $13.50

No. 1398 Antique Gold **Plated** Floor Stand Only, Height of Stand, 62″.
LIST $8.50 EACH.

No. 2356 **Shade** Only, Size 11″x17″,
LIST, $5.00 EACH.

No. 1498/2456 COMPLETE, LIST, $12.00

No. 1498 Antique Gold **Plated** Stand Only. Height of Stand, 59″.
LIST, $8.50 EACH

No. 2456 Shade Only, size 8x11″,
LIST, $3.50 EACH

MODIFIED MODERNISTIC FLOOR AND BRIDGE LAMPS TO MATCH

STANDARD PACKAGE—ANY FOUR

Shades No. 2704 and No. 2804, at the left, are Cocoa Ombre Pleated Georgette with Tangerine Silk Lining, Crushed Velvet Panels.

No. 1487/2804
COMPLETE,
LIST, $21.00

No. 1487
Antique Gold **Plated**
Stand
Height of Stand, 59″
LIST, Stand Only
$12.50 EACH

No. 2804
Shade
Size 10x11x11″
LIST, Shade Only
$8.50 EACH

No. 1387/2704
COMPLETE,
LIST, $27.50

No. 1387
Antique Gold **Plated**
Stand
Height of Stand, 63″
LIST, Stand Only
$12.50 EACH

No. 2704
Floor Shade
Size 16x15x15″
LIST, Shade Only
$15.00 EACH

No. 1389/2703
COMPLETE,
LIST, $27.50

No. 1389
Antique Gold **Plated**
Stand
Height of Stand, 63″
LIST, Stand Only
$12.50 EACH

No. 2703
Shade
Size 10x14x21″
LIST, Shade Only
$15.00 EACH

No. 1489/2803
COMPLETE,
LIST, $21.00

No. 1489
Antique Gold **Plated**
Stand
Height of Stand, 62″
LIST, Stand Only
$12.50 EACH

No. 2803
Shade
Size 8x10x14″
LIST, Shade Only
$8.50 EACH

Shades No. 2703 and No. 2803, at the right, are Crushed Velvet in Varigated Colors, Lined with Gold Satin.

FLOOR AND BRIDGE LAMPS TO MATCH

STANDARD PACKAGE—ANY FOUR

Shades No. 2726 and No. 2826, at the left, are Leatherette with Conventional Design, Red predominating.

No. 1356/2726
COMPLETE,
LIST, $14.00

No. 1356
Silver Polychrome
Stand
Height of Stand, 61″
LIST, Stand Only
$8.50 EACH

No. 2726
Shade
Size 8 x 15
LIST, Shade Only
$5.50 EACH

No. 1456/2826
COMPLETE,
LIST, $12.25

No. 1456
Silver Polychrome
Bridge Stand
Height of Stand, 57″
LIST, Stand Only
$8.50 EACH

No. 2826
Shade
Size 7x10x12″
LIST, Shade Only
$3.75 EACH

No. 1458/2459
COMPLETE,
LIST, $13.50

No. 1458
Antique Gold Stand
Height of Stand, 57″
LIST, Stand Only
$8.50 EACH

No. 2459
Shade
Size 8x11″
LIST, Shade Only
$5.00 EACH

No. 1358/2359
COMPLETE,
LIST, $16 00

No. 1358
Antique Gold
Floor Stand
Height of Stand, 61″
LIST, Stand Only
$8.50 EACH

No. 2359
Shade
Size 11x19″
LIST, Shade Only
$7.50 EACH

Shades No. 2359 and No. 2459, at the right, are Leatherette Parchment with Modernistic Design, Laced, with Red predominating.

FLOOR AND BRIDGE LAMPS TO MATCH

STANDARD PACKAGE—ANY FOUR

Floor Shade No. 2715, at the left, is Blue Ombre Georgette with Embroidered Panels and Italian Glass Fringe; can also furnish same Shade in Mulberry Ombre **No. 2716**, and Cocoa Ombre **No. 2717** at LIST, $20.00

Bridge Shades No. 2817, at the left, is Cocoa Ombre to match above; can also furnish Blue Ombre **No. 2815**, and Mulberry Ombre **No. 2816**.

AT LIST, $12.50

No. 1499/2817 COMPLETE, LIST, $25.00

No. 1499
Antique Gold **Plated** Stand
Height of Stand, 61″
LIST, Stand Only
$12.50 EACH

No. 2817
Cocoa Ombre Shade
Size 8x9x13″
LIST, Shade Only
$12.50 EACH

No. 1399/2715 COMPLETE, LIST, $32.50

No. 1399
Antique Gold **Plated** Stand
Height of Stand, 63″
LIST, Stand Only,
$12.50 EACH

No. 2715
Blue Ombre Shade
Size 15x15x22″
LIST, Shade Only,
$20.00 EACH

> Note: If you want Bridge and Floor Shades of the same color, be sure to order right number.
>
> See other color shades listed above for lamps at the left and below for lamps at the right.

No. 1399/2713 COMPLETE, LIST, $32.50

No. 1399
Antique Gold **Plated** Stand
Height of Stand, 63″
LIST, Stand Only
$12.50 EACH

No. 2713
Mulberry Ombre Shade
Size 21x18x18)
LIST, Shade Only
$20.00 EACH

No. 1499/2812 COMPLETE, LIST, $25.00

No. 1499
Antique Gold **Plated** Stand
Height of Stand, 61″
LIST, Stand Only
$12.50 EACH

No. 2812
Blue Ombre Shade
Size 12x12x12″
LIST, Shade Only
$$12.50 EACH

Floor Shade No. 2713, at the right, is Mulberry Ombre Georgette with Embroidered Panels and Italian Glass Fringe; can also furnish same Shade in Blue Ombre **No. 2712** and Cocoa Ombre **No. 2714**.

AT LIST, $20.00

Bridge Shade No. 2812, at the right, is Blue Ombre to match above; can also furnish Mulberry Ombre **No. 2813**, and Cocoa Ombre **No. 2814**.

AT LIST, $12.50

FLOOR AND BRIDGE LAMPS TO MATCH

STANDARD PACKAGE—ANY FOUR

Shades No. 2725 and **No. 2825**, at the left, are Gesso Leatherette Parchment, Laced, with Brown predominating.

No. 1361/2725 COMPLETE, LIST, $15.00

No. 1361
Green and Gold Stand
Height of Stand, 61″
LIST, Stand Only
$8.50 EACH

No. 2725
Shade
Size 12x17x18″
LIST, Shade Only
$6.50 EACH

No. 1459/2825 COMPLETE, LIST, $12.50

No. 1459
Green and Gold Bridge Stand
Height of Stand, 58″
LIST, Stand Only
$8.50 EACH

No. 2825
Shade
Size 8x11x11″
LIST, Shade Only
$4.00 EACH

No. 1457/2458 COMPLETE, LIST, $13.50

No. 1457
Antique Gold Stand
Height of Stand, 58″
LIST, Stand Only
$8.50 EACH

No. 2458
Shade
Size 8x12x12″
LIST, Shade Only
$5.00 EACH

No. 1357/2358 COMPLETE, LIST, $16.00

No. 1357
Antique Gold Floor Stand
Height of Stand, 61″
LIST, Stand Only
$8.50 EACH

No. 2358
Shade
Size 12x18x18″
LIST, Shade Only
$7.50 EACH

Shades No. 2358 and **No. 2458**, at the right, are Hand-Painted Leatherette Parchment, Laced, with Green predominating.

MODIFIED MODERNISTIC FLOOR AND BRIDGE LAMPS TO MATCH

STANDARD PACKAGE—ANY FOUR

Shades No. 2751 and No. 2851 at the left are Amber Alanoid, Laced Panels.

No. 1465/2851 COMPLETE, LIST $17.50

No. 1465
Antique Copper Bronze Stand
Height of Stand, 59″
LIST, Stands Only, $12.50 EACH

No. 2851
Shade
Size 8x9x13″
LIST, Shade Only, $5.00 EACH

No. 1365/2751 COMPLETE, LIST, $20.00

No. 1365
Antique Copper Plated Stand
Height of Stand, 61″
LIST, Stand Only, $12.50 EACH

No. 2751 Shade
Size 10x15x20″
LIST, Shade Only, $7.50 EACH

No. 1393/2752 COMPLETE, LIST, $20.00

No. 1393 Antique Gold Plated Floor Stand
Height of Stand, 63″
LIST, Stand Only
$12.50 EACH

No. 2752
Shade
Size 10x15x20″
LIST, Shade Only
$7.50 EACH

No. 1493/2852 COMPLETE, LIST, $17.50

No. 1493
Antique Gold Plated Stand
Height of Stand, 61″
LIST, Stand Only, $12.50 EACH

No. 2852 Shade
Size 8x9x13″
LIST, Shade Only, $5.00 EACH

Shades No. 2752 and No. 2852 at the right, are Silver Alanoid with Laced Panels.

MODIFIED MODERNISTIC FLOOR AND BRIDGE LAMPS

STANDARD PACKAGE—ANY FOUR

Shades No. 1774 and No. 1874 are Green Alanoid with Laced Panels.

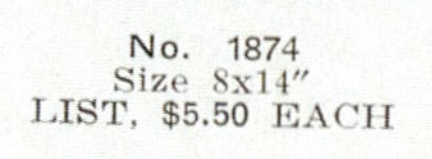
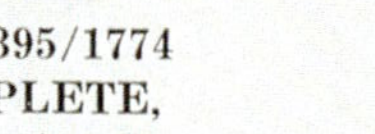

No. 1495/1874 COMPLETE, LIST, $16.00

No. 1495 Tokio Bronze Plated Bridge Stand,
Height of Stand, 59″
LIST, Stand Only
$10.50 EACH

No. 1874
Size 8x14″
LIST, $5.50 EACH

No. 1395/1774 COMPLETE, LIST, $20.00

No. 1395 Tokio Bronze Plated Stand.
Height of Stand, 61″
LIST, Stand Only, $10.50 EACH

No. 1774 Shade
Size 10x22″
LIST, Shade Only,
$9.50 EACH

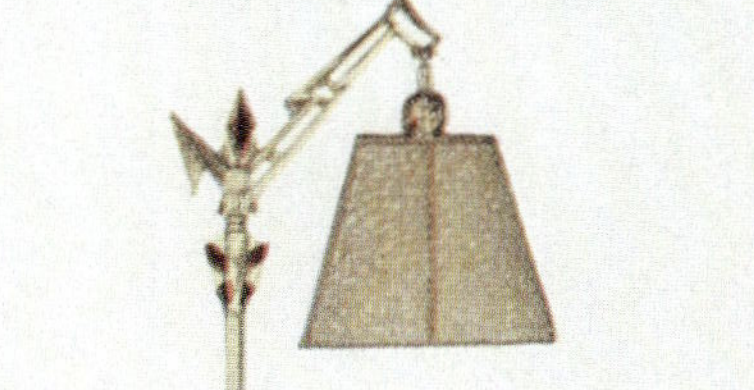

No. 1392/1761 COMPLETE, LIST, $21.50

No. 1392 Antique Gold Plated Floor Stand,
Height of Stand, 59″
LIST, Stand Only,
$12.50 EACH

No. 1761 Shade
Size 11x14x14″
LIST, Shade Only,
$9.00 EACH

No. 1492/899 COMPLETE, LIST, $19.00

No. 1492 Antique Gold Plated Stand
Height of Stand, 60″
LIST, Stand Only,
$12.50 EACH

No. 899 Shade
Size 8x10x10″
LIST, Shade Only,
$6.50 EACH

Shades No. 899 and No. 1761 are Gold Alanoid with Laced Panels.

MODIFIED MODERNISTIC FLOOR AND BRIDGE LAMPS TO MATCH

STANDARD PACKAGE—ANY FOUR

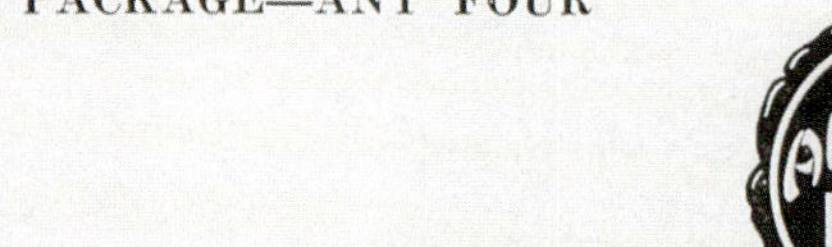

Shades No. 1772 and No. 1872, at the left, are Silver Tinted Alanoid with Hand-Painted Design, and Laced Panels.

No. 1493/1872 COMPLETE, LIST, $18.00

No. 1493
Swedish Iron **Plated**
Bridge Stand
Height of Stand, 60″
LIST, Stand Only
$12.50 EACH

No. 1872
Shade
Size 8x10x10″
LIST, Shade Only
$5.50 EACH

No. 1393/1772 COMPLETE, LIST, $22.50

No. 1393
Swedish Iron **Plated**
Stand
Height of Stand, 62″
LIST, Stand Only
$12.50 EACH

No. 1772
Shade
Size 11x16x16″
LIST, Shade Only
$10.00 EACH

No. 1394/1773 COMPLETE, LIST, $23.00

No. 1394
Swedish Iron **Plated**
Floor Stand
Height of Stand, 62″
LIST, Stand Only
$14.00 EACH

No. 1773
Shade
Size 10x18x18″
LIST, Shade Only
$9.00 EACH

No. 1494/1873 COMPLETE, LIST, $19.00

No. 1494
Swedish Iron **Plated**
Stand
Height of Stand, 58″
LIST, Stand Only
$14.00 EACH

No. 1873
Shade
Size 7x12x12″
LIST, Shade Only
$5.00 EACH

Shades No. 1773 and No. 1873, at the right, are Silver Tinted Alanoid with Hand-Painted Design, Laced Panels.

MODERN FLOOR AND BRIDGE LAMPS

STANDARD PACKAGE—ANY FOUR

Shades No. 1771 and No. 1871 at the left, are Black Ombre Pleated Georgette with Tangerine Silk Lining and Crushed Velvet Panels.

No. 1375/1771 COMPLETE, LIST, $27.50

No. 1375
Ormolu Gold **Plated**
Height of Stand, 58″
LIST, Stand Only,
$16.50 EACH

No. 1771
Size 12x16x16″
LIST, Shade Only,
$16.00 EACH

No. 1475/1871 COMPLETE, LIST, $27.50

No. 1475
Ormolu Gold **Plated**
Height of Stand, 57″
LIST, Stand Only,
$16.50 EACH

No. 1871
Size 9x13x13″
LIST, **$11.00** EACH

No. 1474/1870 COMPLETE, LIST, $32.50

No. 1474
Ormolu Gold **Plated**
Height of Stand, 58″
LIST, Stand Only,
$15.50 EACH

No. 1870
Size 8x11x11″
LIST, Shade Only,
$10.00 EACH

No. 1374/1770 COMPLETE, LIST, $32.50

No. 1374
Ormolu Gold **Plated**
Height of Stand, 60″
LIST, Stand Only,
$17.50 EACH

No. 1770
Size 12x20x20″
LIST, Shade Only,
$15.00 EACH

Shades No. 1770 and No. 1870, at the right, are Satin Modernistic Design, Lined with Silk Tangerine with Crushed Velvet Panels.

MODIFIED MODERNISTIC FLOOR AND BRIDGE LAMPS TO MATCH

STANDARD PACKAGE—ANY FOUR

Shades **No.** 1762 and **No.** 1850, at the left, are Varigated Alanoid Laced Panels with Red and Green predominating.

No. 1485/1850
COMPLETE,
LIST, $17.50

No. 1485
Oxidized Cooper
Plated Bridge Stand
Height of Stand, 61″
LIST, Stand Only
$12.50 EACH

No. 1850
Shade
Size 8x9x13″
LIST, Shade Only
$5.00 EACH

No. 1388/2700
COMPLETE,
LIST, $30.00

No. 1388
Antique Gold **Plated**
Floor Stand
Height of Stand, 63″
LIST, Stand Only
$13.50 EACH

No. 2700
Shade
Size 8x15x19″
LIST, Shade Only
$16.50 EACH

No. 1385/1762
COMPLETE,
LIST, $21.00

No. 1385
Oxidized Copper
Plated Stand
Height of Stand, 63″
LIST, Stand Only
$12.50 EACH

No. 1762
Shade
Size 10x15x20″
LIST, Shade Only
$8.50 EACH

No. 1488/2800
COMPLETE.
LIST, $22.50

No. 1488
Antique Gold **Plated**
Stand
Height of Stand, 60″
LIST, Stand Only
$13.50 EACH

No. 2800
Shade
Size 5x8x12″
LIST, Shade Only
$9.00 EACH

Shades **No.** 2700 and **No.** 2800, at the right, are Pleated Georgette, Black and White Ombre, with Modernistic Alanoid Panels and Satin Lining to match.

MODERN FLOOR AND BRIDGE LAMPS TO MATCH

STANDARD PACKAGE—ANY FOUR

Shades **No.** 1790 and **No.** 1890, at the left, are Tangerine Ombre Pleated Georgette with Tangerine Silk Lining.

No. 1376/1790
COMPLETE,
LIST, $32.50

No. 1376
Ormolu Gold **Plated**
Floor Stand
Height of Stand, 60″
LIST, Stand Only
$16.00 EACH

No. 1790
Shade
Size 10x22″
LIST, Shade Only
$16.50 EACH

No. 1476/1890
COMPLETE,
LIST, $25.00

No. 1476
Ormolu Gold **Plated**
Stand
Height of Stand, 57″
LIST, Stand Only
$15.00 EACH

No. 1890
Shade
Size 8 x 14″
LIST, Shade Only
$10.00 EACH

No. 1477/843
COMPLETE,
LIST, $25.00

No. 1477
Ormolu Gold **Plated**
Bridge Stand
Height of Stand, 57″
LIST, Stand Only
$15.00 EACH

No. 843
Shade
Size 8 x 12″
LIST, Shade Only
$10.00 EACH

No. 1377/1753
COMPLETE,
LIST, $32.50

No. 1377
Ormolu Gold **Plated**
Stand
Height of Stand, 60″
LIST, Stand Only
$15.00 EACH

No. 1753
Shade
Size 12x18″
LIST, Shade Only,
$17.50 EACH

Shades **No.** 1753 and **No.** 843, at the right, are Embroidered Sand Georgette with Pleated Georgette Border and Rose Silk Lining.

MODERN FLOOR AND BRIDGE LAMPS TO MATCH

STANDARD PACKAGE—ANY FOUR

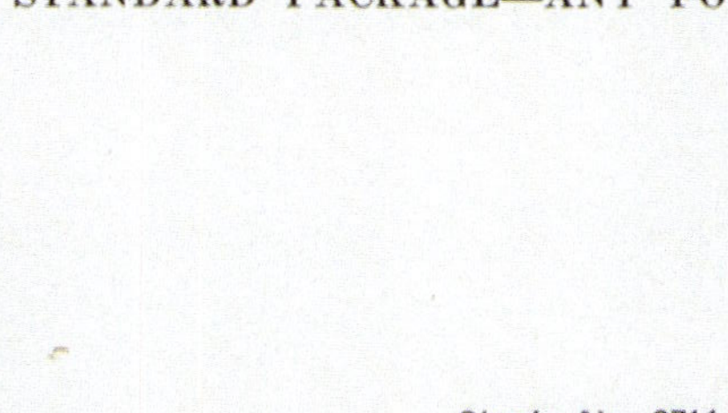

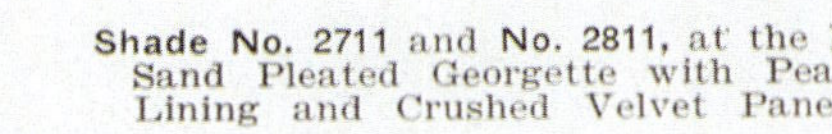

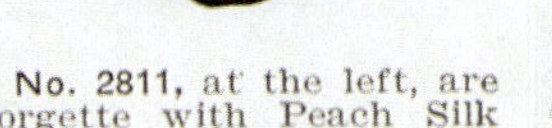

Shade No. 2711 and **No. 2811**, at the left, are Sand Pleated Georgette with Peach Silk Lining and Crushed Velvet Panels.

No. 1490/1869
COMPLETE,
LIST, $25.00

No. 1490
Antique Gold **Plated**
Stand
Height of Stand, 63″
LIST, Stand Only,
$13.50 EACH

No. 1869
Shade
Size 9½x12″
LIST, Shade Only,
$11.50 EACH

No. 1386/2711
COMPLETE,
LIST, $30.00

No. 1386
Antique Gold **Plated**
Stand
Height of Stand, 63″
LIST, Stand Only,
$15.00 EACH

No. 2711
Shade
Size 11x15x20″
LIST, Shade Only,
$15.00 EACH

No. 1390/1769
COMPLETE,
LIST, $30.00

No. 1390
Antique Gold **Plated**
Stand
Height of Stand, 61″
LIST, Stand Only,
$13.00 EACH

No. 1769
Shade
Size 12 x 18″
LIST, Shade Only,
$17.00 EACH

No. 1486/2811
COMPLETE,
LIST, $27.50

No. 1486
Antique Gold **Plated**
Stand
Height of Stand, 59″
LIST, Stand Only,
$15.00 EACH

No. 2811
Shade
Size 9x11x13″
LIST, Shade Only,
$12.50 EACH

Shade No. 1769 and **No. 1869**, at the right, are Gold Satin with Tangerine Silk Lining and Crushed Velvet Panels.

MODERN FLOOR AND BRIDGE LAMPS TO MATCH

STANDARD PACKAGE—ANY FOUR

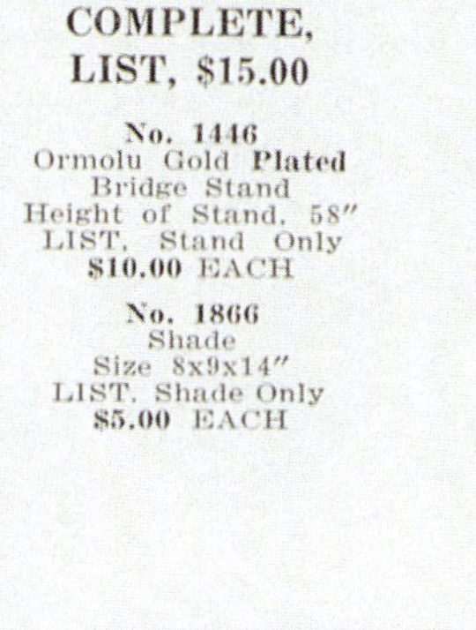

Shades No. 1766 and **No. 1866**, at the left, are Sand Pleated Georgette with Tangerine Silk Lining.

No. 1446/1866
COMPLETE,
LIST, $15.00

No. 1446
Ormolu Gold **Plated**
Bridge Stand
Height of Stand, 58″
LIST, Stand Only
$10.00 EACH

No. 1866
Shade
Size 8x9x14″
LIST, Shade Only
$5.00 EACH

No. 1345/1768
COMPLETE,
LIST, $17.50

No. 1345
Ormolu Gold **Plated**
Floor Stand
Height of Stand, 61″
LIST, Stand Only
$10.00 EACH

No. 1768
Shade
Size 11x13x20″
LIST, Shade Only
$7.50 EACH

No. 1346/1766
COMPLETE,
LIST, $17.50

No. 1346
Ormolu Gold **Plated**
Stand
Height of Stand, 61″
LIST, Stand Only
$10.00 EACH

No. 1766
Shade
Size 11x13x20″
LIST, Shade Only
$7.50 EACH

There are not our best quality Georgette Shades as you can tell by the remarkable low prices, but they are exceptional values at these prices.

No. 1445/1868
COMPLETE,
LIST, $15.00

No. 1445
Ormolu Gold **Plated**
Stand
Height of Stand, 58″
LIST, Stand Only
$10.00 EACH

No. 1868
Shade
Size 7x9x14″
LIST, Shade Only
$5.00 EACH

Shades No. 1763 and **No. 1868**, at the right, are Rose Pleated Georgette with Rose Silk Lining.

FLOOR AND BRIDGE LAMPS TO MATCH

STANDARD PACKAGE—ANY FOUR

Shades No. 2702 and **No. 2802** are Green Faille Silk, Tangerine Silk Lining, Embroidered Taffeta Panels and Italian Glass Fringe.

No. 1384/2702 COMPLETE, LIST, $35.00

No. 1384 Ormolo Gold **Plated** Stand
Height of Stand, 65″
LIST, Stand Only
$12.50 EACH

No. 2702 Shade
Size 12 x 14 x 20
LIST, Shade Only,
$22.50 EACH

No. 1484/2802 COMPLETE, LIST, $25.00

No. 1484 Ormolo Gold **Plated** Stand
Height of Stand, 62″
LIST, Stand Only
$12.50 EACH

No. 2802
Shade
Size 7x9x14″
LIST, Shade Only
$12.50 EACH

No. 1491/2801 COMPLETE, LIST, $25.00

No. 1491 Antique Gold **Plated** Stand
Height of Stand, 62″
LIST, Stand Only
$12.50 EACH

No. 2801 Shade
Size 8x10x14″
LIST, Shade Only,
$12.50 EACH

No. 1391/2701 COMPLETE, LIST, $37.50

No. 1391 Antique Gold **Plated** Stand
Height of Stand, 65″
LIST, Stand Only
$12.50 EACH

No. 2701
Shade
Size 12x15x22″,
LIST, Shade Only
$25.00 EACH

Shades No. 2701 and **No. 2801** are Tan Faille Silk, Tangerine Silk Lining, Crushed Velvet Panels and Italian Glass Fringe.

FLOOR AND BRIDGE LAMPS TO MATCH

STANDARD PACKAGE—ANY FOUR

Shades are Hand-Painted Beaded Cloth with Glass Fringe.

No. 390/887 COMPLETE, LIST, $24.00

No. 390 Tokio Bronze
Stand Only,
Height of Stand, 61″
LIST, $9.00 EACH.

No. 887 Shade Only,
Size 15 x 21″,
LIST, $15.00 EACH.

No. 490/877 COMPLETE, LIST, $18.00

No. 490 Tokio Bronze,
Bridge Stand Only,
Height of Stand, 59″
LIST, $9.00 EACH.

No. 877 Shade Only,
Size 8x10x14″,
LIST, $9.00 EACH.

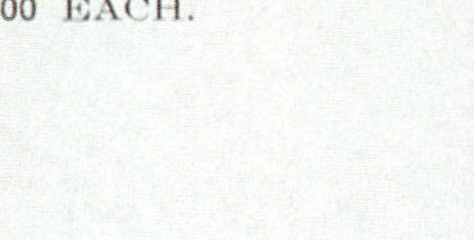

No. 393/886 COMPLETE, LIST, $24.00

No. 393 Antique Gold
Floor Stand Only,
Height of Stand, 61″.
LIST, $9.00 EACH.

No. 866 **Shade** Only,
Size 15 x 20″,
LIST, $15.00 EACH.

No. 493/876 COMPLETE, LIST, $18.00

No. 493 Antique Gold Stand Only,
Height of Stand, 59″.
LIST, $9.00 EACH.

No. 876 Shade Only, Size 10x10x14″,
LIST, $9.00 EACH.

"ALADDIN" END TABLE LAMPS

STANDARD PACKAGE—ANY SIX

Shades are Hand-Painted, Beaded, with Black Velvet Binding. Size, 8 x 9".

LIST, Shades Only, $2.50 EACH

No. 312/722
BLACK
GLAZE
LIST, $7.50

No. 313/723
ROSE MATT
LIST, $7.50

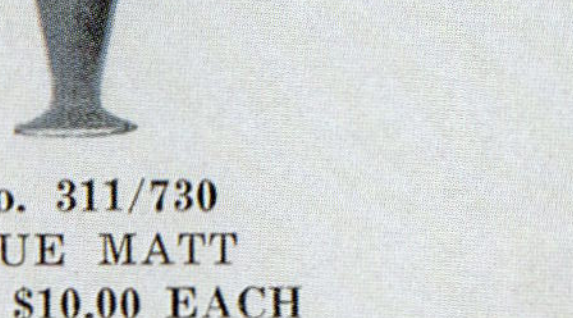

No. 311/721
BLUE MATT
LIST, $7.50

Stands are One Light. Height, 20"

LIST, Stands Only, $5.00 EACH

"ALADDIN" POTTERY END TABLE LAMPS

STANDARD PACKAGE—ANY SIX

Shade No. 730 Orchid Georgette Pleated over Lavender Silk Mull.

Shade No. 732 Coral Georgette Pleated over Gold Silk Mull.

Shade No. 731 Green Georgette Pleated over Peach Mull.

Size 8 x 8 x 12"

LIST, Shades Only, $5.00 EACH.

No. 311/730
BLUE MATT
LIST, $10.00 EACH

No. 313/732
ROSE MATT
LIST, $10.00 EACH

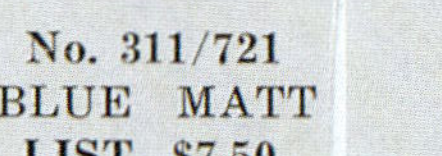

No. 312/731
BLACK GLAZE
LIST, $10.00 EACH

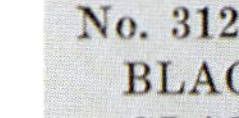

Stands are One Light, Genuine Pottery.

Height, 20"

LIST Stands Only, $5.00 EACH.

"ALADDIN" MODERN TABLE LAMPS

STANDARD PACKAGE—ANY THREE

Shade. Diameter, 16″
LIST, Shades Only, $7.50 EACH

No. 1335/1745
GOLD CRINKLED
LIST, $15.00

No. 1336/1746
SILVER CRINKLED
LIST, $15.00

No. 1337/1747
RUSSET CRINKLED
LIST, $15.00

Stand, Height, 20″
LIST, Stands Only, $7.50 EACH

"ALADDIN" MODERN TABLE LAMPS

STANDARD PACKAGE—ANY SIX

Shades No. 1706, 1708, 1727 are Hand-Painted Leatherette Parchment, size 10½ x 16″.
LIST Price, Shades Only, $4.00 EACH.

No. 1312/1727
DECORATED BLACK
LIST, $10.00 EACH

No. 1313/1708
DECORATED BLACK
LIST, $10.00 EACH

Stands 1311, 1312, 1313, are Black Crinkled Glass, Hand-Decorated, with Metal Plated Mounting. Height, 20″.

LIST Price, Stands Only, $6.00 EACH.

No. 1311/1706
DECORATED BLACK
LIST, $10.00 EACH

"ALADDIN" END TABLE LAMPS

STANDARD PACKAGE—ANY SIX

Shades are Hand-Painted Glass.
Diameter, 10″

LIST, Shades Only, $3.00 EACH

No. 348/975
NILE IVORY TINTED
LIST, $7.50

No. 348/976
NILE IVORY TINTED
LIST, $7.50

No. 348/977
NILE IVORY TINTED
LIST, $7.50

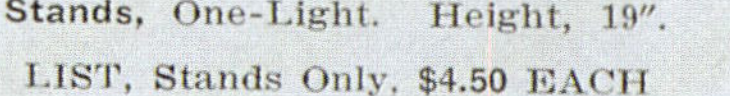

Stands, One-Light. Height, 19″.
LIST, Stands Only, $4.50 EACH

"ALADDIN" TABLE LAMPS

STANDARD PACKAGE—ANY THREE

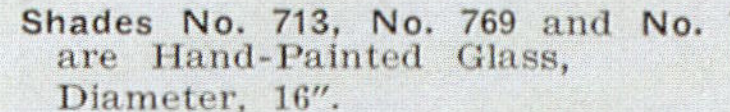
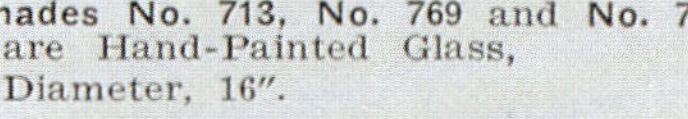

Shades No. 713, No. 769 and No. 714 are Hand-Painted Glass,
Diameter, 16″.

LIST, Shades Only, $8.25 EACH.

No. 323/713
CYRIAN BRONZE
LIST, $15.00 EACH

No. 486/769
ANTIQUE GOLD
LIST, $15.00 EACH

Stands, Cast Metal, Two-Light,
Height, 20″.
LIST, Stands Only, $6.75 EACH

No. 314/714
GOLD POLYCHROME
LIST, $15.00 EACH

"ALADDIN" TABLE LAMPS

STANDARD PACKAGE—ANY THREE

Shades No. 890, 1700, and 1701 are Hand-Painted Glass, Diameter 18".

LIST, Shades Only, $10.25 EACH.

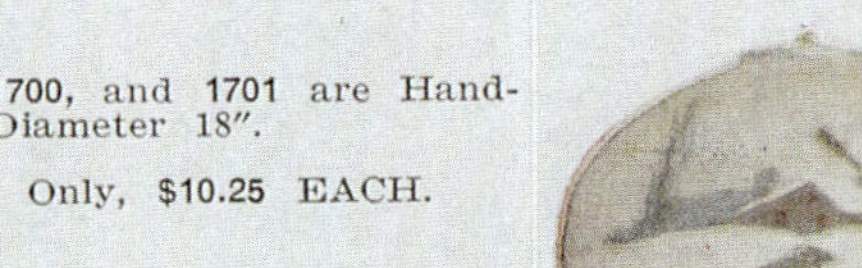

No. 1327/890
PARISIAN BRONZE
LIST, $18.50 EACH

No. 1326/1701
DECORATED
LIGHT VERDE
LIST, $18.50 EACH

No. 1328/1700
POLYCHROME
LIST, $18.50 EACH

Stands, Cast Metal Two-Light, Height, 22".

LIST, Stands Only, $8.25 EACH.

"ALADDIN" TABLE LAMPS

STANDARD PACKAGE—ANY THREE

SHADES No. 700, 798, and No. 799 are Hand-Painted Glass, Diameter, 14".

LIST, Shades Only, $6.00 EACH.

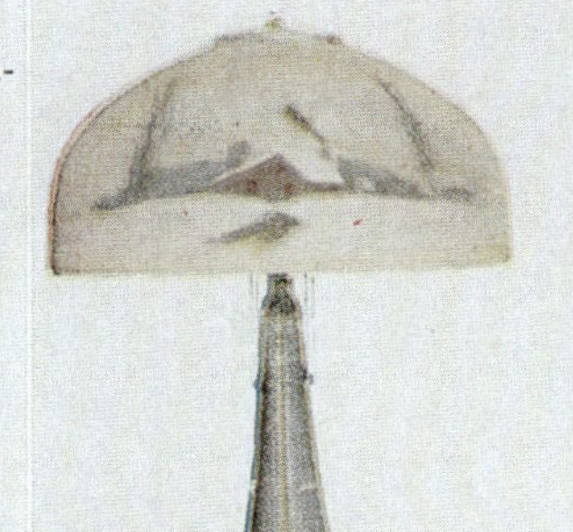

No. 481/604
BLUE BRONZE
LIST, $12.50 EACH

No. 323/798
CORSICAN BRONZE
LIST, $12.50 EACH

No. 398/799
PARISIAN BRONZE
LIST, $12.50 EACH

Stand, Cast Metal, Height, 19".

LIST, Stand Only, $6.50 EACH.

"ALADDIN" TABLE LAMPS

STANDARD PACKAGE—ANY THREE

Shades No. 589, **No.** 768, and **No.** 979 are Hand-Painted Glass. Diameter, 16″.

LIST, Shades Only, $8.25 EACH

No. 314/589
GOLD POLYCHROME
LIST, $15.00 EACH

No. 400/768
EGYPTIAN BRONZE
LIST, $17.00 EACH

No. 528/979
MANDARIN BRONZE
LIST, $16.00 EACH

Stands, Cast Metal, Two-Light. Height, 21″.

LIST, Stands Only, **No.** 314, $6.75; **No.** 400, $8.75; **No.** 528, $7.75 EACH.

"ALADDIN" BEAUTIFUL VANITY LAMPS

STANDARD PACKAGE—ANY SIX

Shade No. 1662 Rose Faille Silk with Rose China Silk Stretched Lining Finished with Lace. Size 8″x10″.
LIST, Shade Only, $5.50 EACH.

Shade No. 1660 Gold Silk with Gold China Silk Stretched Lining Finished with Lace and Gold Ribbon. Size 8″ x 10″.
LIST, Shade Only, $7.50 EACH.

Shade No. 1661 Green Silk with Peach China Silk Stretched Lining Finished with Ruching to Match. Size 8″ x 10″.
LIST, Shade Only, $6.50 EACH.

No. 1261/1662
ROSE
LIST, $8.00 EACH

No. 1262/1660
FAWN
LIST, $10.00 EACH

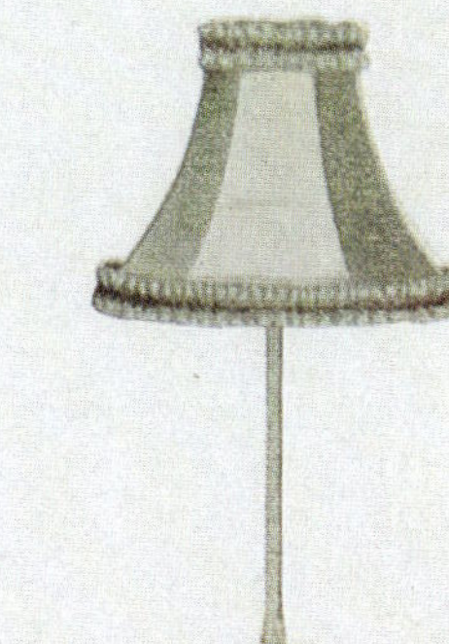

No. 1260/1661
PALE PEA GREEN
LIST. $9.00 EACH

Stands, Cast Metal and Brass Tubing. Height, 16″.

LIST, Stands Only, $2.50 EACH.

"ALADDIN" BOUDOIR LAMPS

STANDARD PACKAGE—ANY SIX

Shade No. 1666 Orange Ombre Georgette, Gold China Silk Lining.

Shade No. 1667 Sand Georgette Pleated, Rose China Silk Stretched Lining.

Shade No. 1668 Green Georgette Pleated, Peach China Silk Stretched Lining.

Size 6 x 9"

LIST, Shades Only, $4.75 EACH

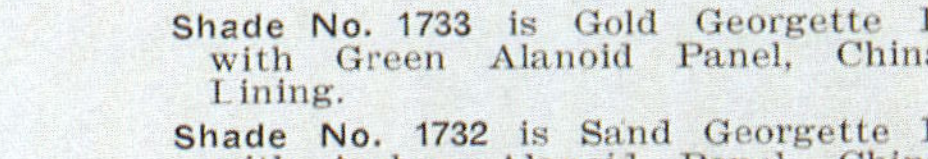

No. 277/1666
IVORY AND TAN
LIST, $7.50

No. 278/1667
OLIVE AND BROWN
LIST, $7.50

No. 279/1668
IVORY AND GREEN
LIST, $7.50

Stands, Height, 14".

LIST, Stands Only, $2.75 EACH

"ALADDIN" MODERN TABLE LAMPS

STANDARD PACKAGE—ANY THREE

Shade No. 1733 is Gold Georgette Pleated with Green Alanoid Panel, China Silk Lining.

Shade No. 1732 is Sand Georgette Pleated with Amber Alanoid Panel, China Silk Lining.

Shade No. 1734 is Brown Ombre Georgette Pleated with Amber Alanoid Panel, China Silk Lining.

Shades, Size 9½ x 15"

LIST, Shades Only, $12.50 EACH

No. 1334/1733
BLUE CRINKLED
LIST, $17.50

No. 1332/1732
LAVENDER BRONZE
CRINKLED
LIST, $17.50

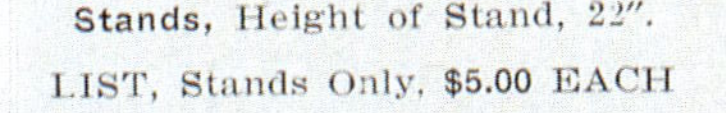

No. 1333/1734
BLACK CRINKLED
LIST, $17.50

Stands, Height of Stand, 22".

LIST, Stands Only, $5.00 EACH

"ALADDIN" TABLE LAMPS

STANDARD PACKAGE—ANY SIX

Shades are Hand-Painted Parchment, with Black Velvet Binding. Size 9 x 17"

LIST, Shades Only, $2.50 EACH

No. 336/813
Black with Embossed Bird Decoration
LIST, $7.50

No. 336/812
Black with Embossed Bird Decoration
LIST, $7.50

No. 336/811
Black with Embossed Bird Decoration

Stand, Two-Light. Height, 20".

LIST, Stands Only, $5.00 EACH

"ALADDIN" END TABLE OR BOUDOIR LAMPS

STANDARD PACKAGE—ANY SIX

Shade No. 824 Green, Georgette Pleated over Yellow Silk.

Shade No. 825 Coral Georgette Pleated over Peach Silk.

Shade No. 826 Orchid Georgette Pleated over Peach Silk.

Size $7\frac{1}{2}$ x $10\frac{1}{2}$"

LIST, Shade Only, $3.50 EACH.

No. 308/824
OAK BUFF TINTED
LIST, $7.00 EACH

No. 308/825
OAK BUFF TINTED
LIST, $7.00 EACH

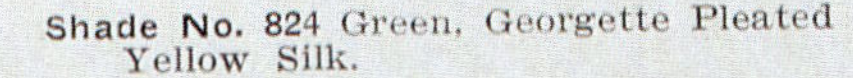

No. 308/826
OAK BUFF TINTED
LIST, $7.00 EACH

Stands, Cast White Metal, Height, 14",

LIST, **Stands** Only, $3.50 EACH.

"ALADDIN" JEWEL CASE BOUDOIR LAMPS

STANDARD PACKAGE—ANY SIX

Shade No. 1663 Orchid Georgette Pleated, Peach Silk Lining.

Shade No. 1665 Green Embroidered Georgette, Gold Satin Lining.

Shade No. 1664 Coral Georgette Pleated, Peach Silk Lining.
Size, 7 x 7 x 10"

LIST, Shades Only, $4.75 EACH

No. 1226/1663
PARISIAN BRONZE
LIST, $8.75

No. 1226/1665
PARISIAN BRONZE
LIST, $8.75

No. 1226/1664
PARISIAN BRONZE
LIST, $8.75

"ALADDIN" BOUDOIR LAMPS

Stand, 12" High, LIST, $2.00 EACH. **Shades,** Diameter 7", LIST, $2.50.

STANDARD PACKAGE—ANY TWELVE

LIST, $4.50 EACH

283/610 BLACK Green Georgette Shade	285/611 ROSE Coral Georgette Shade	284/612 BLUE Orchid Georgette Shade

STANDS ARE LUSTER WITH CAST METAL MOUNTING

SET No. 9202—12 Assorted [4 Each as Shown Above] List, $48.00 for 12
Shipping Weight, 30 Lbs.

Stand, 12" High, LIST, $2.00 EACH. **Shade,** Diameter 8", LIST, $2.00 EACH.

STANDARD PACKAGE—ANY TWELVE

LIST, $4.00 EACH

283/685 BLACK	284/684 BLUE	285/683 ROSE

SHADES ARE HAND-PAINTED PARCHMENT

STANDS ARE LUSTER WITH CAST METAL MOUNTING

"ALADDIN" BOUDOIR LAMPS

Stand, 13″ High, LIST $2.25 EACH — Shade Diameter 6″, LIST $2.25

STANDARD PACKAGE—ANY TWELVE

LIST, $4.50 EACH

254/678	253/677	255/676
ROSE	BLUE	IVORY

SHADES ARE HAND-PAINTED PARCHMENT—STANDS CAST METAL.

SET No. 9352—12 Assorted [4 Each as Shown Above] List $54.00 for 12

Shipping Weight, 40 Lbs.

Stand 13″ High, LIST $1.90 EACH — Shade Diameter 6″, LIST $ .60 EACH

STANDARD PACKAGE—ANY TWELVE

LIST, $2.50 EACH

1200/1605	220/1604	219/1603
IVORY AND BROWN	GOLD	IVORY

SHADES ARE HAND-PAINTED PARCHMENT—STANDS CAST METAL.

"ALADDIN" SPECIAL METAL BOUDOIR LAMPS

Stand, 13″ High, LIST, $3.50 EACH. — Shade, Diameter 8½″, LIST, $2.50 EACH.

STANDARD PACKAGE—ANY TWELVE

LIST, $6.00 EACH

289/658	288/656	271/657
PLATED GREEN & BRONZE	PLATED SILVER & BLACK	PLATED ANTIQUE GOLD

SHADES ARE HAND-PAINTED GLASS CRINKLED FINISH—STANDS CAST METAL

SET No. 9264—12 Assorted [4 Each as Shown Above] List, $72.00 for 12

Shipping Weight, 50 Lbs.

Stand, 14″ High, LIST, $2.75 EACH. — Shade, Diameter 8½″, LIST, $1.75 EACH.

STANDARD PACKAGE—ANY TWELVE

LIST, $4.50 EACH

277/1047	279/1048	278/1049
IVORY AND TAN	IVORY AND GREEN	OLIVE AND BROWN

SHADES ARE HAND-PAINTED GLASS CRINKLED FINISH—STANDS CAST METAL

"ALADDIN" BOUDOIR LAMPS

Stand, 13" High, LIST, $1.75 EACH. Shade Diameter 6", LIST, $ .75 EACH.

STANDARD PACKAGE—ANY TWELVE
LIST $2.50 EACH

234/665	224/666	233/667
Green and Gold	Old Ivory	Blue and Bronze

SHADES ARE GLASS HAND-PAINTED—STANDS CAST METAL.

SET No. 9236—12 Assorted [4 Each as Shown Above] List, **$30.00 for 12**
Shipping Weight, 40 Lbs.

"ALADDIN" BOUDOIR LAMPS

Stand, 14" High, LIST, $2.00 EACH. Shades, Diameter 8", LIST, $1.50 EACH.

STANDARD PACKAGE—ANY TWELVE
LIST, $3.50 EACH

256/634	257/632	258/629
OLD IVORY	RUSSET BRONZE	OLD IVORY

SHADES ARE GLASS HAND-PAINTED—STANDS CAST METAL

SET No. 9351—12 Assorted [4 Each as Shown Above] List, **$42.00 for 12**
Shipping Weight, 55 Lbs.

Stand, 13" High, LIST, $1.75 EACH. Shade Diameter 5½", LIST, $ .75 EACH.

STANDARD PACKAGE—ANY TWELVE
LIST, $2.50 EACH

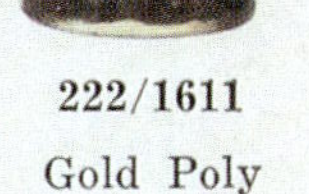

222/1610	222/1609	222/1611
Gold Poly	Gold Poly	Gold Poly

SHADES ARE GLASS HAND-PAINTED—STANDS CAST METAL.

Stand, 13" High, LIST, $1.75 EACH. Shade, Diameter 5½", LIST, $ .75 EACH.

STANDARD PACKAGE—ANY TWELVE
LIST, $2.50 EACH

219/681	222/679	236/680
OLD IVORY	GOLD POLYCHROME	LAVENDER

SHADES ARE GLASS HAND-PAINTED—STANDS CAST METAL

"ALADDIN" BOUDOIR LAMPS

Stand, 13″ High, LIST, $1.60 EACH. Shades, Diameter, 5½″, LIST, $ .65 EACH.

STANDARD PACKAGE—ANY TWELVE
LIST, $2.25 EACH

1200/1602 OLD IVORY

1200/1600 OLD IVORY

1200/1601 OLD IVORY

SHADES ARE GLASS HAND-PAINTED—STANDS CAST METAL.

SET No. 9247—12 Assorted [4 Each as Shown Above] List, **$27.00** for 12

Shipping Weight, 40 Lbs.

Stand, 13″ High, LIST, $1.50 EACH. Shades, Diameter 5½″, LIST, $ .50 EACH.

STANDARD PACKAGE—ANY TWELVE
LIST, $2.00 EACH

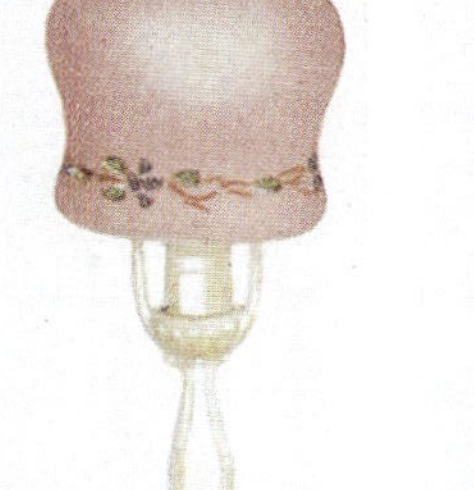

1201/1607 IVORY

1201/1608 IVORY

1201/1606 IVORY

SHADES ARE GLASS HAND-PAINTED—STANDS CAST METAL.

"ALADDIN" PIANO AND RADIO LAMPS

STANDARD PACKAGE—ANY SIX

Shade No. 671 Hand-Painted, Beaded, 7″. LIST, $2.50 EACH

Shade No. 668 Hand-Painted, Glass, 7″. LIST, $2.00 EACH

Shade No. 672 Green Georgette, 7″. LIST, $3.00 EACH

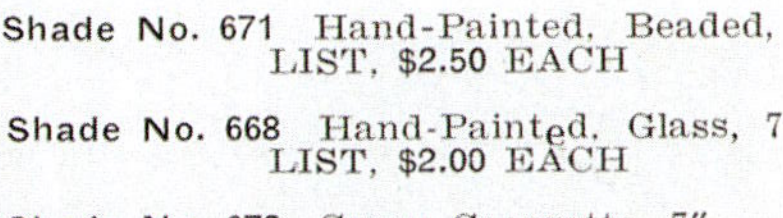

No. 237/671
PARISIAN
LIST, $6.00

No. 238/668
POMP POLY BRONZE
LIST, $5.50

Stands, Adjustable to 12″
LIST, $3.50 EACH

No. 239/672
ITALIAN POLY
LIST, $6.50

All "ALADDIN" Piano and Radio Lamps are Packed in Individual Cartons

"ALADDIN" PIANO, RADIO, AND DESK LAMPS

STANDARD PACKAGE—ANY SIX

Shades No. 755, No. 505, and No. 756 are Hand-Painted Glass, Length 8½".
LIST, Shade Only, $2.50 EACH.

No. 108/755
POMPEIAN BRONZE
LIST, $8.50 EACH

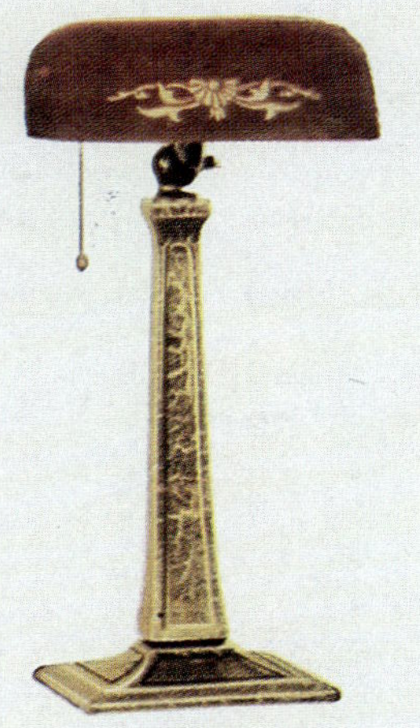

No. 105/505
ANTIQUE GOLD
LIST, $9.00 EACH

No. 109/756
VERDE GREEN
LIST, $8.50 EACH

All "ALADDIN" Piano, Radio, and Desk Lamps are Packed in Individual Cartons.

"ALADDIN" DELUXE-A-LITE DESK LAMPS

No. 79
POMPEIAN BRONZE
Height 18" Standard Package, 3
LIST, $15.00 EACH

No. 76
VERDE GREEN
POMPEIAN BRONZE or
ANTIQUE GOLD
Height, 10"
Standard Package, 6
LIST, $8.50 EACH

No. 111/511
POMPEIAN BRONZE
$10.00 EACH
No. 112/511
[Same as Above Except with Single Inkwell]
LIST, $10.00 EACH
No. 113/511
[Same as above Except with Square New Haven Clock]
LIST $15.00 EACH

No. 750 Shades Only, Green Glass, with White Glass Lining,

LIST, $2.50 EACH

When ordering Shades Only, for Lamps you have, Specify whether you want them

[With hole in each end]

[A hole in one end and slot in the other]

[Or without any holes.]

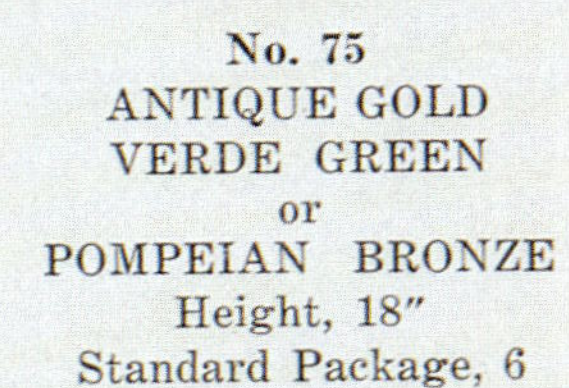

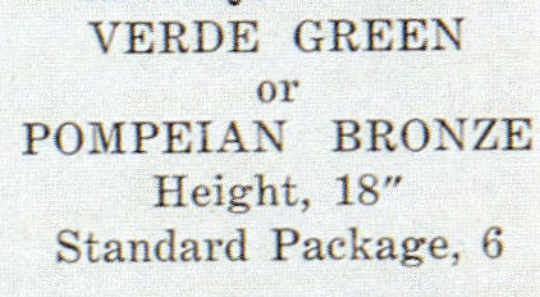

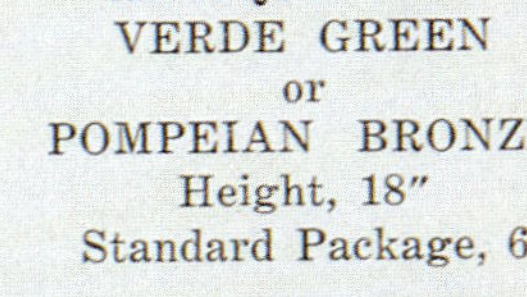

No. 75
ANTIQUE GOLD
VERDE GREEN
or
POMPEIAN BRONZE
Height, 18"
Standard Package, 6
LIST, $9.00 EACH

"ALADDIN" SUPERIOR DESK LAMPS

PLATED FINISHES

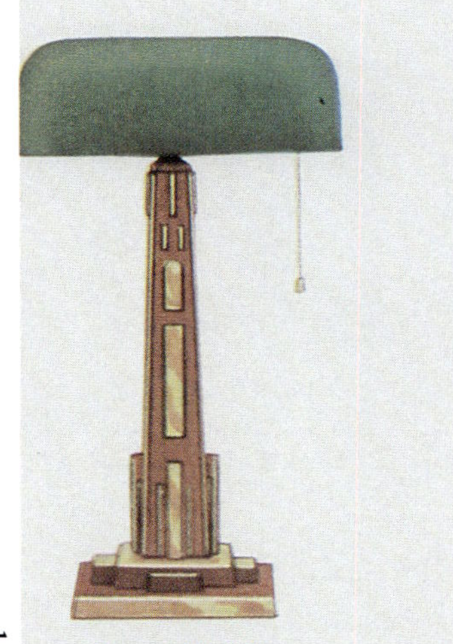

No. 120/704
Antique Gold Plated

No. 122/704
Statuary Bronze Plated

No. 121/704
Gun Metal and Green Plated

Height, 18″
Standard Package, Any 6

LIST, Shades Only,
$3.00 EACH

LIST, COMPLETE,
$10.00 EACH

No. 114/514

Statuary Bronze Plated
Cut and Polished Inkwells

Height, 18″
Standard Package, 3

LIST, Shade Only
$3.00 EACH

LIST, COMPLETE,
$17.50 EACH

No. 1966

Statuary Bronze Plated
Double Adjustable

Height, 6 to 14″
Standard Package, 6

LIST, COMPLETE,
$7.50 EACH

"ALADDIN" DESK LAMPS

STANDARD PACKAGE—ANY SIX

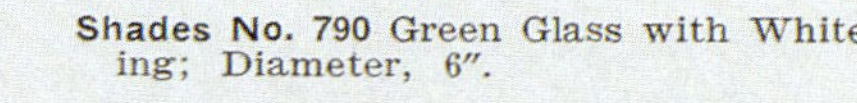

Shades No. 790 Green Glass with White Lining; Diameter, 6″.

LIST, Shade Only, $1.00 EACH.

No. 616

POMPEIAN BRONZE

LIST, $4.25 EACH

No. 584

POMPEIAN BRONZE

LIST, $4.00 EACH

No. 574

POMPEIAN BRONZE

LIST, $4.50 EACH

All "ALADDIN" Desk Lamps Packed in Individual Cartons.

"ALADDIN" BED LAMPS

STANDARD PACKAGE—ANY TWELVE

No. 960 Bed Lamp
(Wired Complete)

Coral Georgette with Gold Lining

Size 5½ x 10″

LIST, $5.00

These are HAND-MADE Georgette Bed Lamps of quality and are not to be compared with the cheap imitation on the market.

No. 961 Bed Lamp
(Wired Complete)

Green Georgette with Peach Lining

Size 5½ x 10″

LIST, $5.00

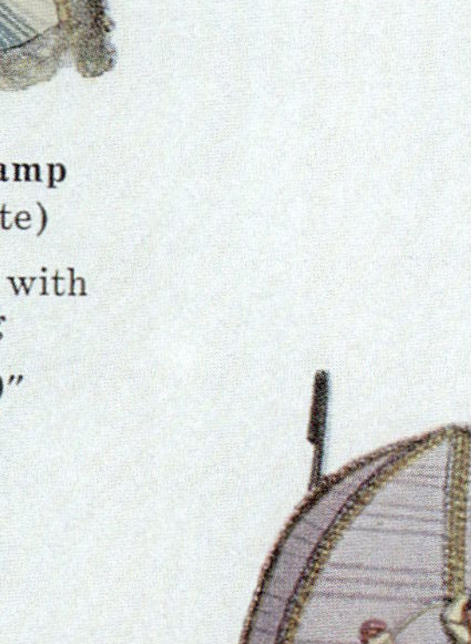

No. 962 Bed Lamp
(Wired Complete)

Orchid Georgette with Lavender Lining

Size 5½ x 10″

LIST, $5.00

Note: These Bed Lamps are COMPLETE with PULL-CHAIN sockets, 9-ft. Silk No. 18 Underwriters Approved Parallel Cord and TWO-PIECE Plug.

SET No. 9981—12 Assorted [2 Each as Shown Above] List, **$60.00** for 12
Shipping Weight, 15 Lbs.

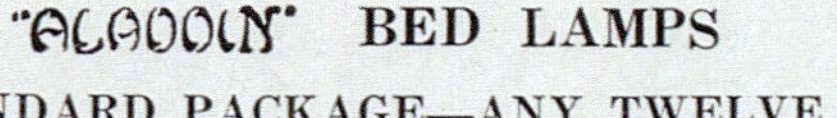

"ALADDIN" BED LAMPS

STANDARD PACKAGE—ANY TWELVE

No. 950 Bed Lamp
(Wired Complete)

Blue, Hand-Painted Beaded Cloth

Size, 5½ x 10″

LIST, $4.00

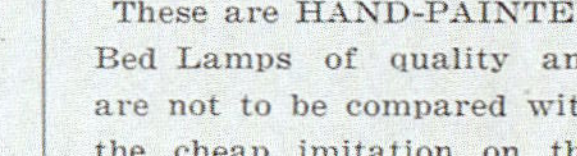

These are HAND-PAINTED Bed Lamps of quality and are not to be compared with the cheap imitation on the market.

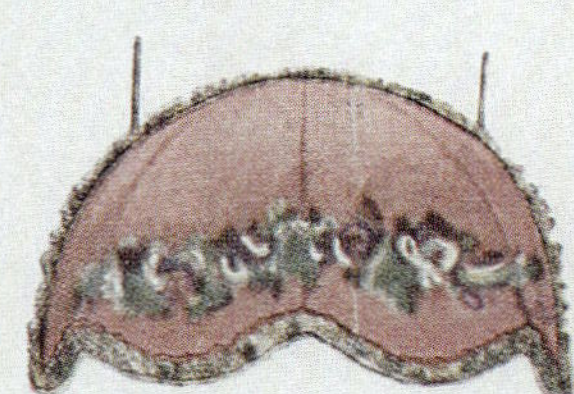

No. 951 Bed Lamp
(Wired Complete)

Pink Hand-Painted Beaded Cloth

Size, 5½ x 10″

LIST, $4.00

Note: These Bed Lamps are COMPLETE with PULL-CHAIN sockets, 9-ft. Silk No. 18 Underwriters Approved Parallel Cord and TWO-PIECE Plug.

No. 952 Bed Lamp
(Wired Complete)

Gold Hand-Painted Beaded Cloth

Size 5½ x 10″

LIST, $4.00

SET No. 9980—12 Assorted [4 Each as Shown Above] List, **$48.00** for 12
Shipping Weight, 30 Lbs.

HANDEL Lamps
IN the making of these unusual lamps, every device of the artist-craftsman is brought into full play. The search for the motif; the choice of pleasing lines which shall bring the base in harmony with the shade; the fashioning of the durable materials, and finally the hand decorating of the shade, make them art objects of permanent attractiveness.
Beautiful and Useful
The Library Table Lamp in the illustration to the left is No. 6637—a lamp of decorative value as well as utility.
Handel Lamps are sold by a dealer near you. We can send you his name. Ask him to show you Handel Lamps.
6641 Library Table Lamp
6672 Boudoir Lamp
6668 Boudoir Lamp
6372 Desk or Piano Lamp
6519 Library Table Lamp
THE HANDEL COMPANY
382 EAST MAIN STREET
MERIDEN, CONN.

Macbeth-Evans Iridile Portable, Number 4515

Beautiful Light in the Home

We make every kind of glassware for illumination — for decorative uses, for efficiency, and for a desirable compromise between the two.

Riddle

DECORATIVE LIGHTING FITMENTS

Smaller Riddle Lamps and Novelties

Top Row

No. 603—Boudoir Lamp. Height 17 inches with 10-inch oval Vellumesque shade. Price $12.50.

No. 634—Console Stick, 22 inches high, shown as pair with Server, No. 7208, in center. Price of Sticks, $40 pair. Server, $10.

No. 600—Boudoir Lamp. Height 16 inches with 10-inch Vellumesque shade. Price $17.50.

Center Row

No. 650—Table Lamp, left, height 25 inches with 18-inch Vellumesque shade. Price $40.

No. 636—Boudoir Lamp with Shade, $9.

No. 652—Table Lamp, right, height 24 inches, with 18-inch Vellumesque shade. Price $37.50.

Bottom Row

No. 7221—Book Blocs, at left, pair $10.

No. 649—Table Lamp. Height 24 inches, with 18-inch Vellumesque shade. Price $35.

No. 7219—Book Blocs, at right, pair $6.

No. 640 No. 8214 No. 642 No. 628 No. 627 No. 614 No. 625

No. 640—Torchere with six decorated candles. Height, 72 inches. Price $125 pair.

No. 8214—Aquarium in Gold Estofado, with beautiful topaz glass bowl with hand fused royal purple border. Height 39 inches. Price $100.

No. 642—Bridge lamp with 15-inch silk-fringed Vellumesque shade. Height 46 inches to bottom of shade, which is adjustable to angle, with half swing arm. Price, with shade, $75.

No. 628—Luminor with Vellumesque lantern. Height 72 inches. Price $100 pair. Appropriate for use in hall.

Riddle

LAMPS, TORCHERES and LUMINORS

No. 627—Chairside lamp with Vellumesque shade. Height 63 inches. Price, with shade, $37.50. A most acceptable style for the living-room.

No. 614—Floor lamp with Vellumesque shade. Height 63 inches. Price, with shade, $75.

No. 625—Floor lamp with Vellumesque shade. Height 51 inches. Arm adjusts shade to angle. Price, with shade, $35.00.

All Riddle lamps are wrought of metal and decorated in the beautiful Silver Estofado. They are wired, complete with heavy silk cord and attachment plug. Your dealer will be glad to show you Riddle Lamps. If unable to secure through a dealer, you may order direct.

STYLE
ALMCO
SERVICE
QUALITY
The ART LAMP MFG. CO.
CHICAGO.

REPRODUCED by the courtesy of the Good Furniture Magazine. From a setting designed in their studios using ALMCO Lamp No. 300. This lamp with its splendid carving, finished in Italian Polychrome and its fine proportions might have been fashioned by the cunning hand of the Renaissance craftsman. The shaft covering is of imported figured green silk velour. Shade No. 347-L-24″ of verdi green taffeta by Schumacher & Co. of New York. Stippled silk moss and heavy eight-inch gold silk fringe, hand shaded to harmonize. Drum lining of champagne silk and innerlining of rose silk. Carefully hand tailored.

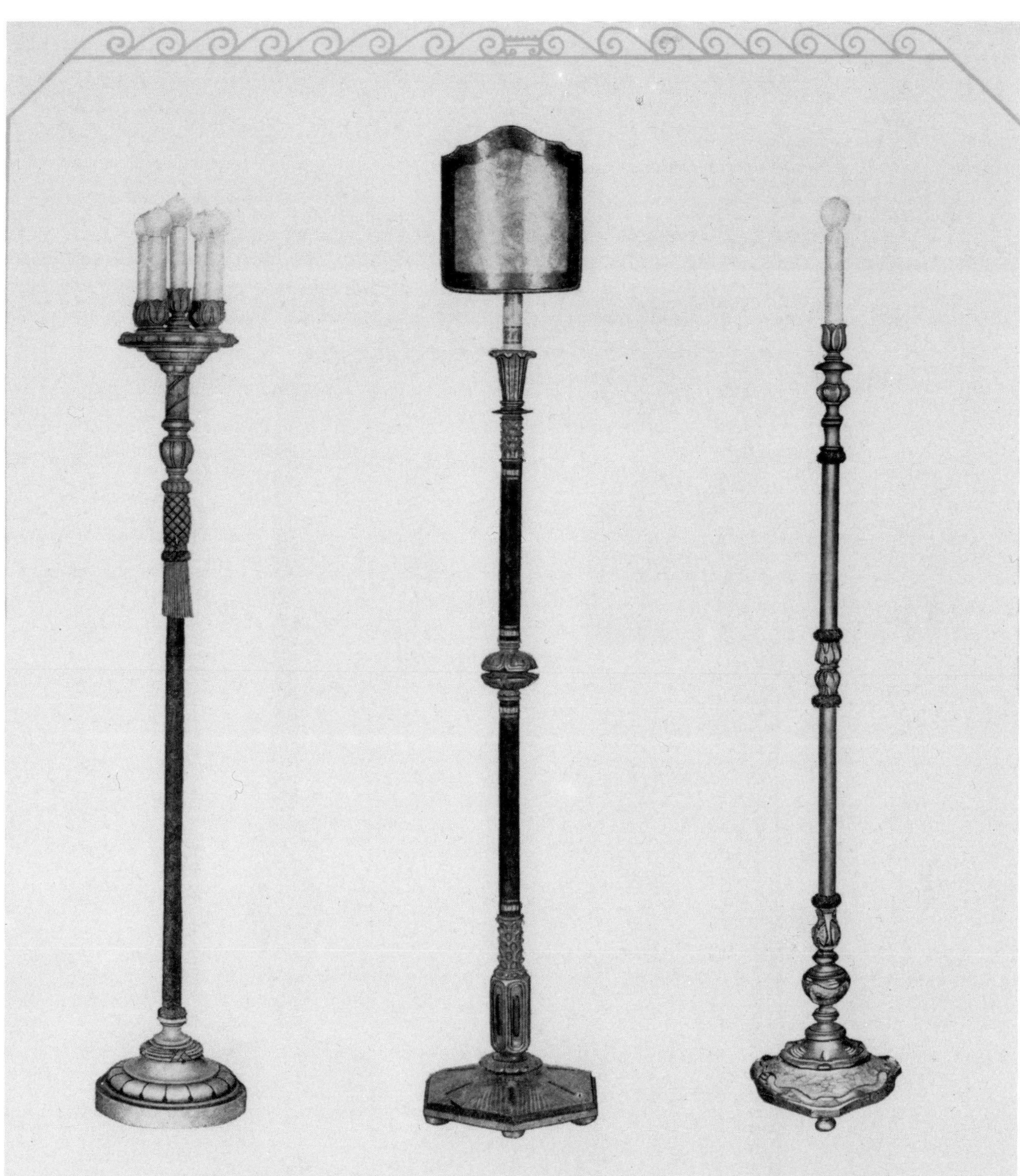

Five Light Torchere No. 189

Finely hand carved. Finished in gold or silver polychrome. Shaft covered with velour of black, blue or mulberry with tassel fringe to match. Completely wired.

Torchere No. 924

Exquisitely hand carved of early gothic style. Polychromed in old gold. Shaft covered in rich red velvet and gold braid.

Mitex Shield No. 1016-1-11

Shield of pure selected mica of soft rich color. Old blue border with antique gold braid.

Torchere No. 236

Richly hand carved with Italian Polychrome finish. Shaft covered in orchid velour and moss. May be had in Antique Gold. Wired with fibre candle.

Regulation Floor Lamp No. 1900

Hand carved and fluted shaft. Finished in gold or silver polychrome. Completely wired.

Shade No. 85-1-26″

Stretched covering of gold and orchid figured silk and gold net. Drum lining of rose. Rich antique gold galoon braid. 6″ grey chenille fringe and orchid tassels.

Regulation Floor Lamp No. 9261

Strictly hand carved with fluted shaft. Dull finish of Mahogany.

Shade No. 390-B-26″

Pleated mulberry silk covering. 6″ Mulberry fringe and skirt. Gold ruching top and bottom. Drum lining of gold silk.

Torchere No. 919

Soft opaque colored polychrome shaft of interesting design. Quaint tallow drip cup. 6" fibre candle and imitation Venetian marble base.

Lantern No. 2036

Japanese lacquer. Black with raised design. Hand decorated glass panels, lined with silk. Colors of silk, rose, gold or blue.

Torchere No. 935

Classical Italian detail with finish of gold and black polychrome. Italian scroll work decorations. 6" fibre candle.

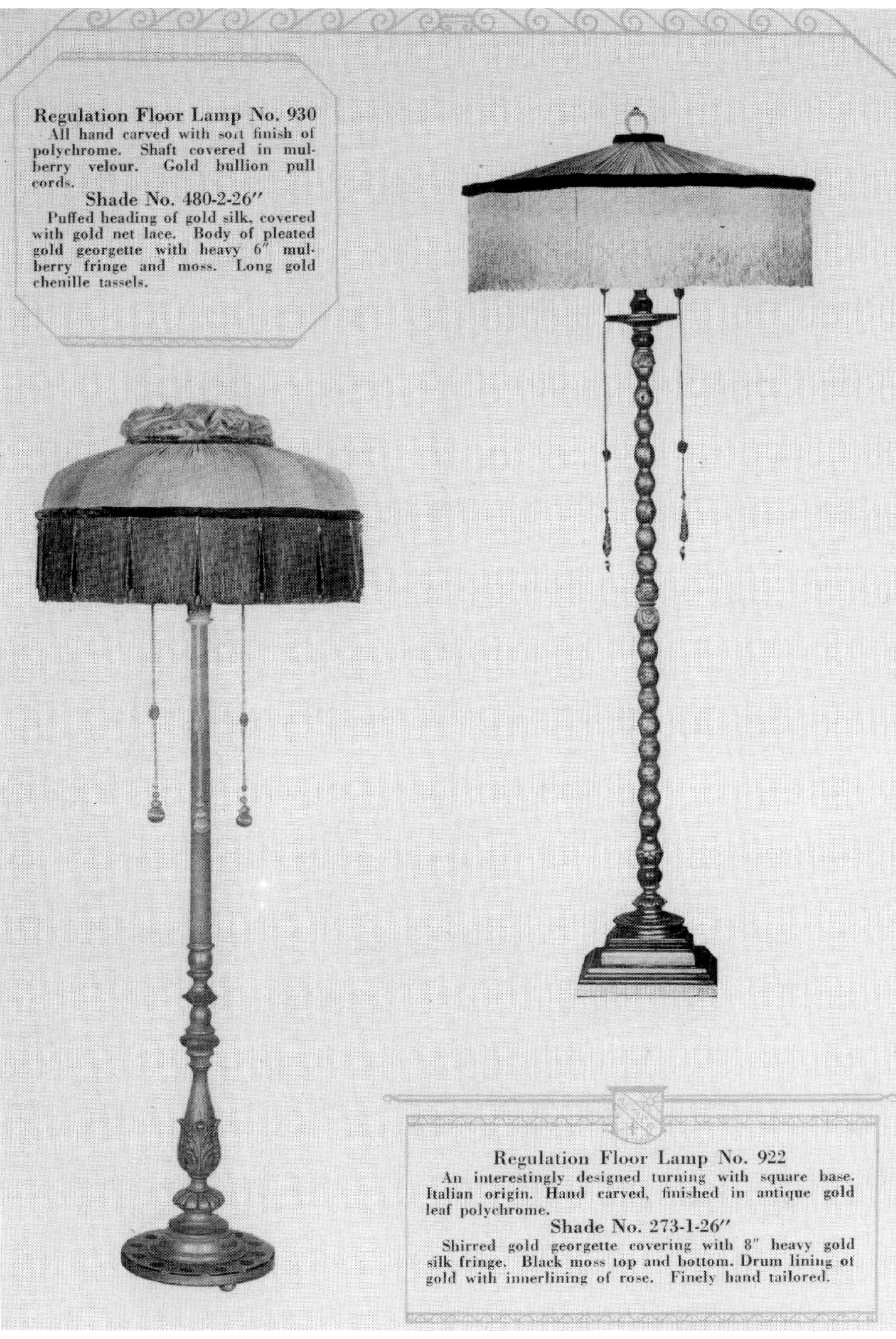

Regulation Floor Lamp No. 930

All hand carved with soft finish of polychrome. Shaft covered in mulberry velour. Gold bullion pull cords.

Shade No. 480-2-26″

Puffed heading of gold silk, covered with gold net lace. Body of pleated gold georgette with heavy 6″ mulberry fringe and moss. Long gold chenille tassels.

Regulation Floor Lamp No. 922

An interestingly designed turning with square base. Italian origin. Hand carved, finished in antique gold leaf polychrome.

Shade No. 273-1-26″

Shirred gold georgette covering with 8″ heavy gold silk fringe. Black moss top and bottom. Drum lining of gold with innerlining of rose. Finely hand tailored.

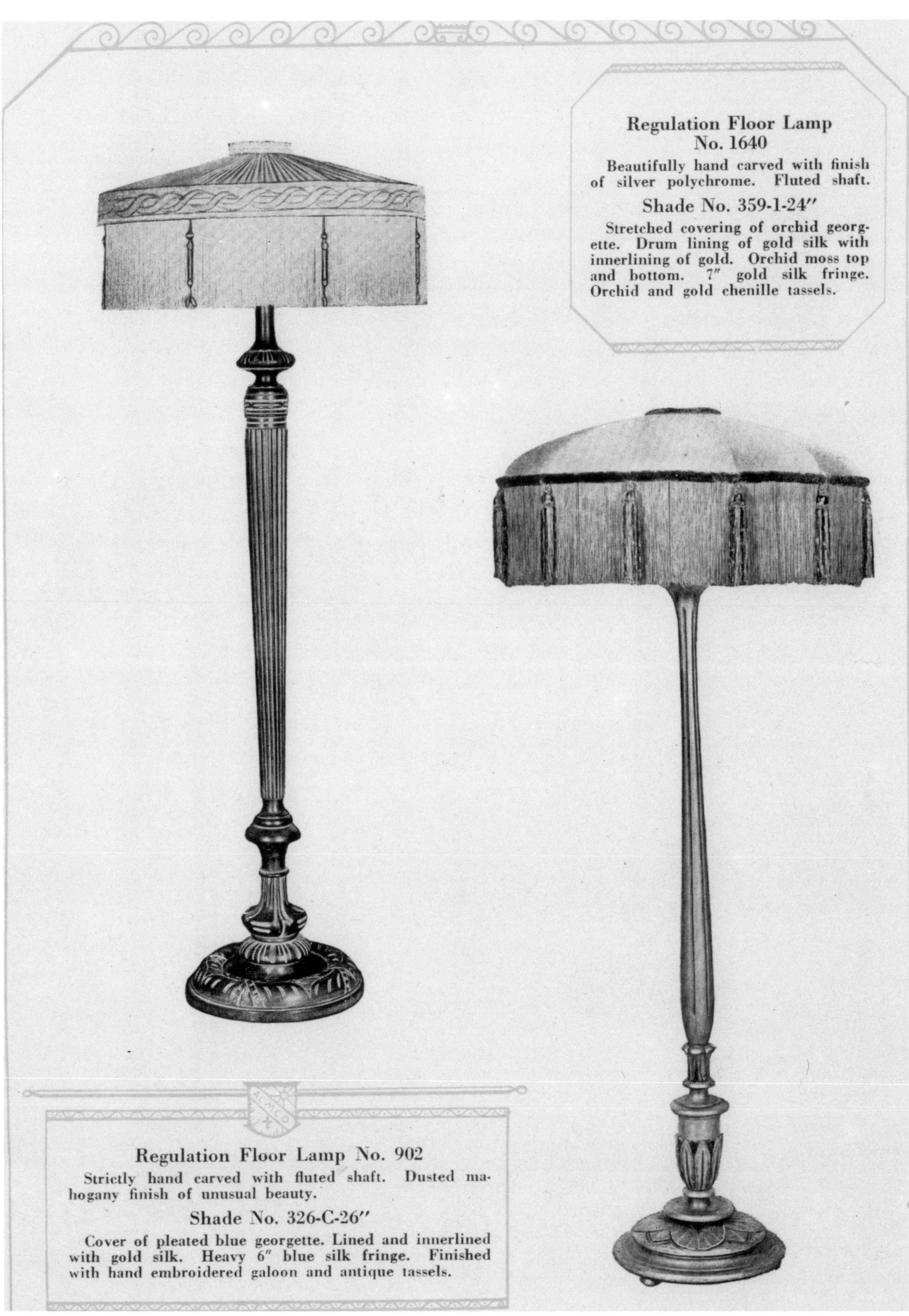

Regulation Floor Lamp No. 1640

Beautifully hand carved with finish of silver polychrome. Fluted shaft.

Shade No. 359-1-24″

Stretched covering of orchid georgette. Drum lining of gold silk with innerlining of gold. Orchid moss top and bottom. 7″ gold silk fringe. Orchid and gold chenille tassels.

Regulation Floor Lamp No. 902

Strictly hand carved with fluted shaft. Dusted mahogany finish of unusual beauty.

Shade No. 326-C-26″

Cover of pleated blue georgette. Lined and innerlined with gold silk. Heavy 6″ blue silk fringe. Finished with hand embroidered galoon and antique tassels.

Regulation Floor Lamp No. 2009

Mahogany finish. Completely wired with two light wireless cluster.

Shade No. 460-C-26″

Covered in silk and chiffon, cut-outs underneath cover. Trimmed with French roses. Silk skirt underneath 6″ silk fringe. Lined in silk mull. Colors: Champ. and Blue; Rose and Gold and Mulb. and Champ.

Regulation Floor Lamp No. 2022

Soft mahogany finish, completely wired ready for use

Shade No. 82-1-26″

Figured blue and gold stretched silk with gold net covering. Lining of rose silk. Wide gold lace galoon with 6″ blue chenille fringe. Black tassels.

Semi-Junior Floor Lamp No. 943

Standard of classical Italian lines. Entirely hand carved with finish of dull hammered gold and black. Wood turning for top of shade. Black velour covering for shaft with cords and tassels to match.

Skintex Shade No. 26-2-24″

Allover design covers top, and with bird among leaves. Vase design on every other side panel. Center of vase has Onyx setting. Gimp of old gold. Blue silk fringe.

Junior Floor Lamp No. 235

Beautifully hand carved gold polychrome finish. Shaft covered in mulberry velour.

Shade No. 560-H-24″

Stretched gold silk covering with mulberry strips over each rib. Old rose lining, mulberry moss, 6″ mulberry silk fringe over gold skirt.

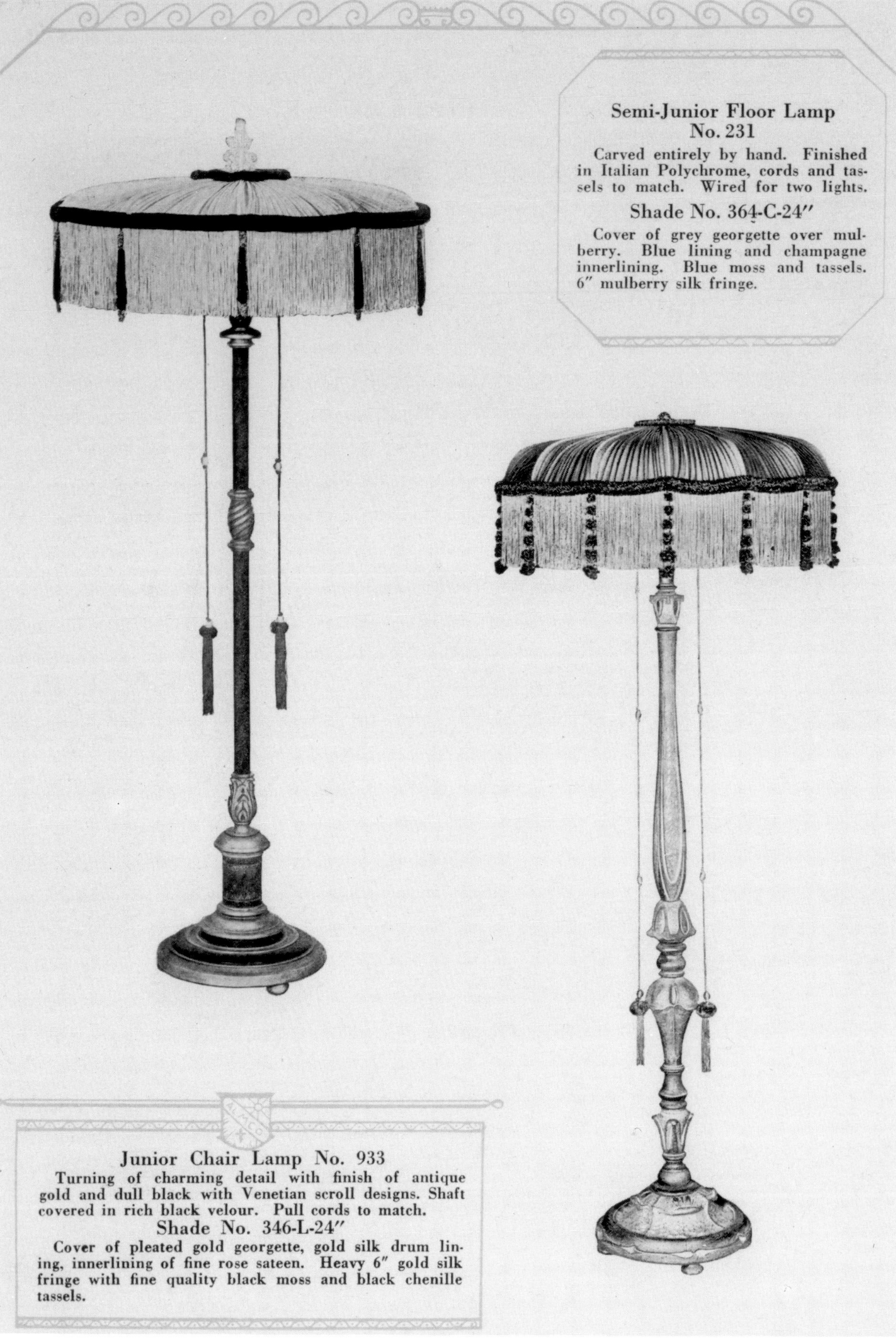

Semi-Junior Floor Lamp No. 231

Carved entirely by hand. Finished in Italian Polychrome, cords and tassels to match. Wired for two lights.

Shade No. 364-C-24″

Cover of grey georgette over mulberry. Blue lining and champagne innerlining. Blue moss and tassels. 6″ mulberry silk fringe.

Junior Chair Lamp No. 933

Turning of charming detail with finish of antique gold and dull black with Venetian scroll designs. Shaft covered in rich black velour. Pull cords to match.

Shade No. 346-L-24″

Cover of pleated gold georgette, gold silk drum lining, innerlining of fine rose sateen. Heavy 6″ gold silk fringe with fine quality black moss and black chenille tassels.

Bridge Lamp No. 928

Beautifully hand carved with twist shaft and acanthus leaf motif. Antique gold polychrome finish. Gracefully shaped bracket finished to harmonize.

Shade No. 40-1-12″

Covering of puffed mauve taffeta. Lining of stretched orchid and orchid innerlining. Mauve silk skirt. Very dainty. Carefully tailored.

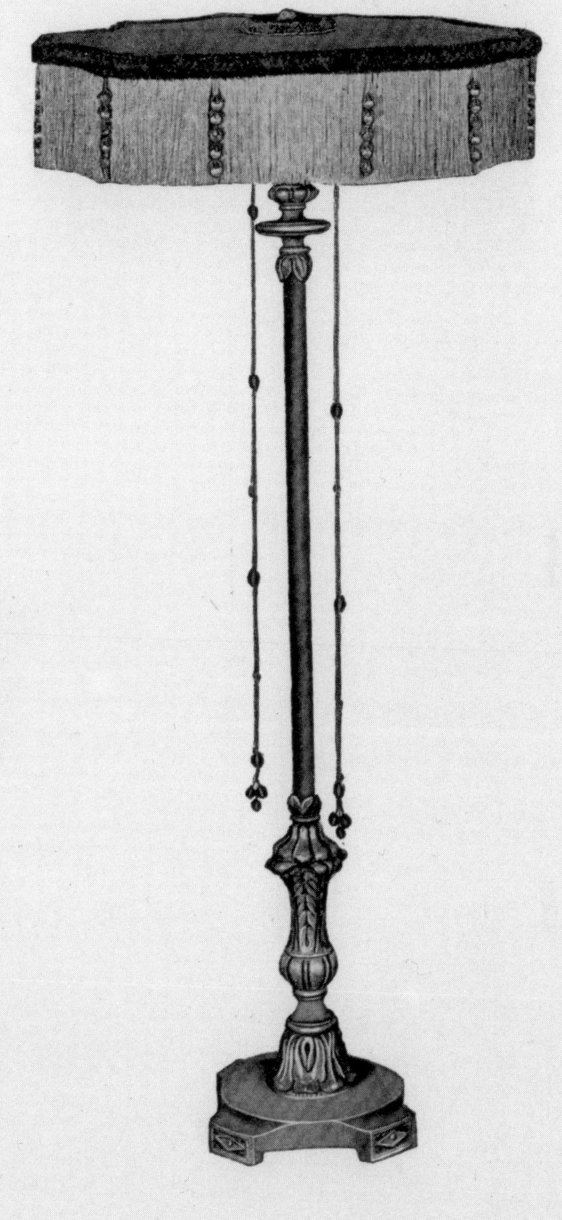

Semi-Junior Floor Lamp No. 240½

Richly hand carved lamp of unusual design. Finished in old silver. Shaft covering of blue velour. Cords and tassels to match.

Shade No. 360-B-24″

Stretched cover of grey silk. Heavy blue moss. 6″ grey silk fringe. Blue tassels. Drum lining of grey silk innerlined with rose.

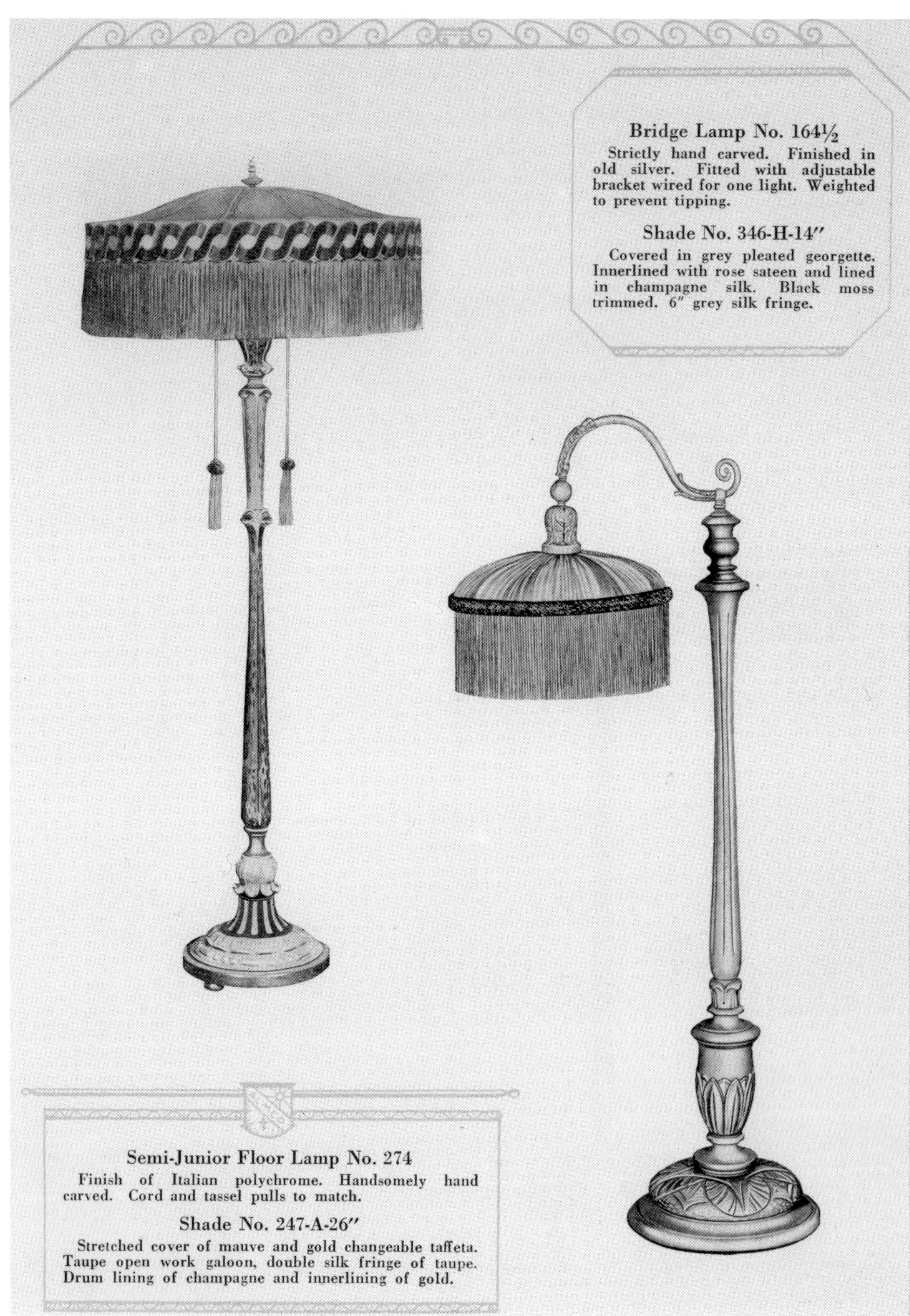

Bridge Lamp No. 164½

Strictly hand carved. Finished in old silver. Fitted with adjustable bracket wired for one light. Weighted to prevent tipping.

Shade No. 346-H-14″

Covered in grey pleated georgette. Innerlined with rose sateen and lined in champagne silk. Black moss trimmed. 6″ grey silk fringe.

Semi-Junior Floor Lamp No. 274

Finish of Italian polychrome. Handsomely hand carved. Cord and tassel pulls to match.

Shade No. 247-A-26″

Stretched cover of mauve and gold changeable taffeta. Taupe open work galoon, double silk fringe of taupe. Drum lining of champagne and innerlining of gold.

Introducing the ALMCO Lamp Suite

Illustrating the development of one design into all types of lamps.

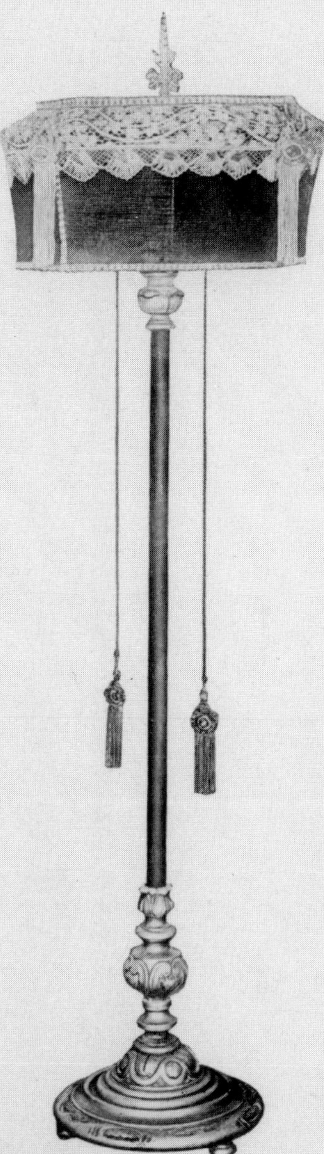

Davenport Lamp No. 224

Finish in antique silver. Hand carved. Orchid velour on shaft. Completely wired.

Shade No. 102-C-9″

Covering of gray georgette shirred over hand painted flowers on wisteria silk. Rose silk lining. Orchid moss, silver ball tassels.

Junior Chair Lamp No. 222

Hand carved, finished in gold polychrome. Black velour on shaft with cords and tassels to match shade. Completely wired.

Shade No. 208-A-16″

Handsomely covered with Black velour. Gorgeous antique silver lace heading, with gold bullion tassels. Stretched gold silk lining with innerlining of American Beauty silk.

Bracket Lamp No. 222

Handsomely hand carved. Finished in silver. Shaft covered with velour of black. Double adjustable bracket of rich design. Completely wired.

Shade No. 346-H-14″

Covering of gray georgette pleated. Champagne lining and innerlining of rose sateen. 6″ gray silk fringe. Heavy black moss top and bottom.

A New Feature for Your Lamp Department

You are sure to please your most particular trade with this selection to choose from.

Davenport Lamp No. 225

Strictly hand carved with finish of Italian polychrome. Use at each end of davenport table.

Shade No. 101-A-9"

Covering of grey georgette with alternate panels stretched and pleated. Lining of grey with innerlining of rose. Black and rose moss with tassels of champagne and blue.

Junior Chair Lamp No. 222

Beautifully hand carved. Solid mahogany, finished in Italian polychrome. Shaft covered in orchid velour, with long cords and tassels to match.

Shade No. 347-A-24"

Covering of gray stretched taffeta with hand painted flowers. Champagne lining and innerlining of rose. 6" grey silk fringe. Heavy orchid moss, with orchid and champagne tassels.

Table Lamp No. 223

Hand carved with a finish of silver polychrome. Orchid velour on shaft and cords and tassels to match. Completely wired.

Shade No. 347-G-20"

Shirred covering of champagne georgette. Lining of champagne and innerlining of blue. Heavy orchid moss 6" champagne silk fringe. Hand tailored.

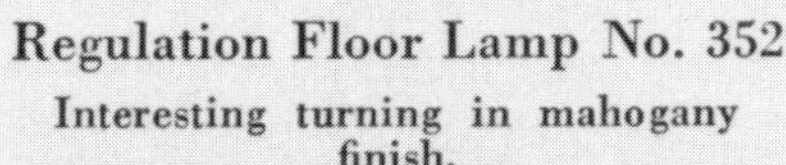

Regulation Floor Lamp No. 352

Interesting turning in mahogany finish.

Skintex Shade No. 774-1-26″

Decorated transparent leather panels alternated with panels of changeable mulberry taffeta shirred to sunburst effects. Mulberry silk fringe and beautiful hand made tassels.

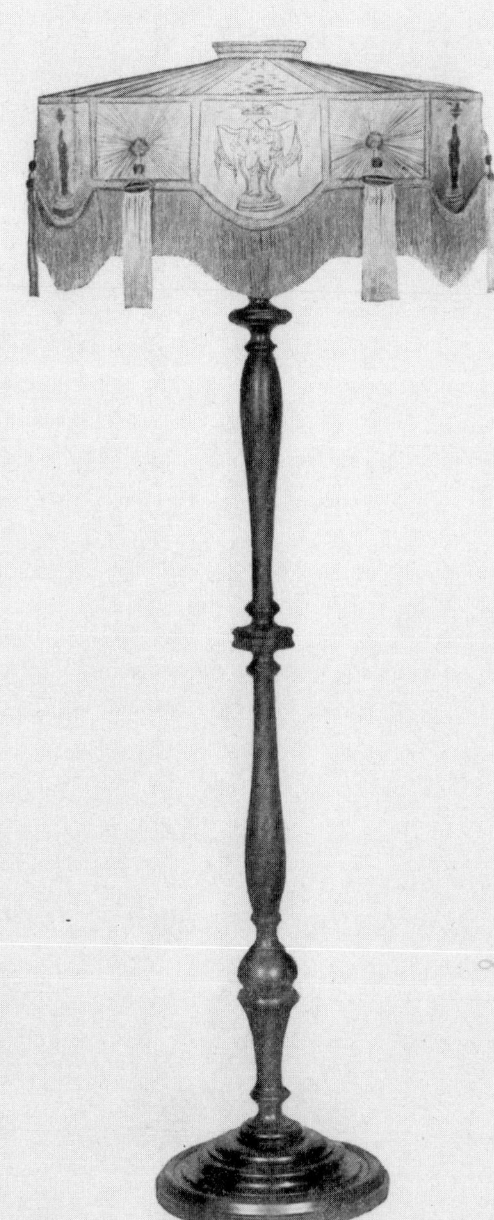

Semi-Junior Floor Lamp No. 2520

Cyrillian blue enamel finish with gold stripes. Soft velvet glazed surface. Blue and champagne cords and tassels.

Skintex Shade No. 208-1-16″

Oriental Turkish design. Brilliant well toned color, giving bright lighting effect. Top and bottom roll of old gold lace. Gimp of gold to match lace.

Semi-Junior Floor Lamp No. 267

A very unusual turning or rich detail. Finished in brown mahogany.

Shade No. 560-Y-26″

Covering of pleated champagne georgette. Lining and innerlining of gold. 6″ black silk fringe over champagne skirt, carefully hand tailored.

Semi-Junior Floor Lamp No. 251

Lustrous mahogany finish. Completely wired.

Shade No. 22-4-26″

Pleated mulberry georgette covering, with lining and innerlining or gold silk. Mulberry and gold galloon. 6″ mulberry silk fringe. All hand tailored.

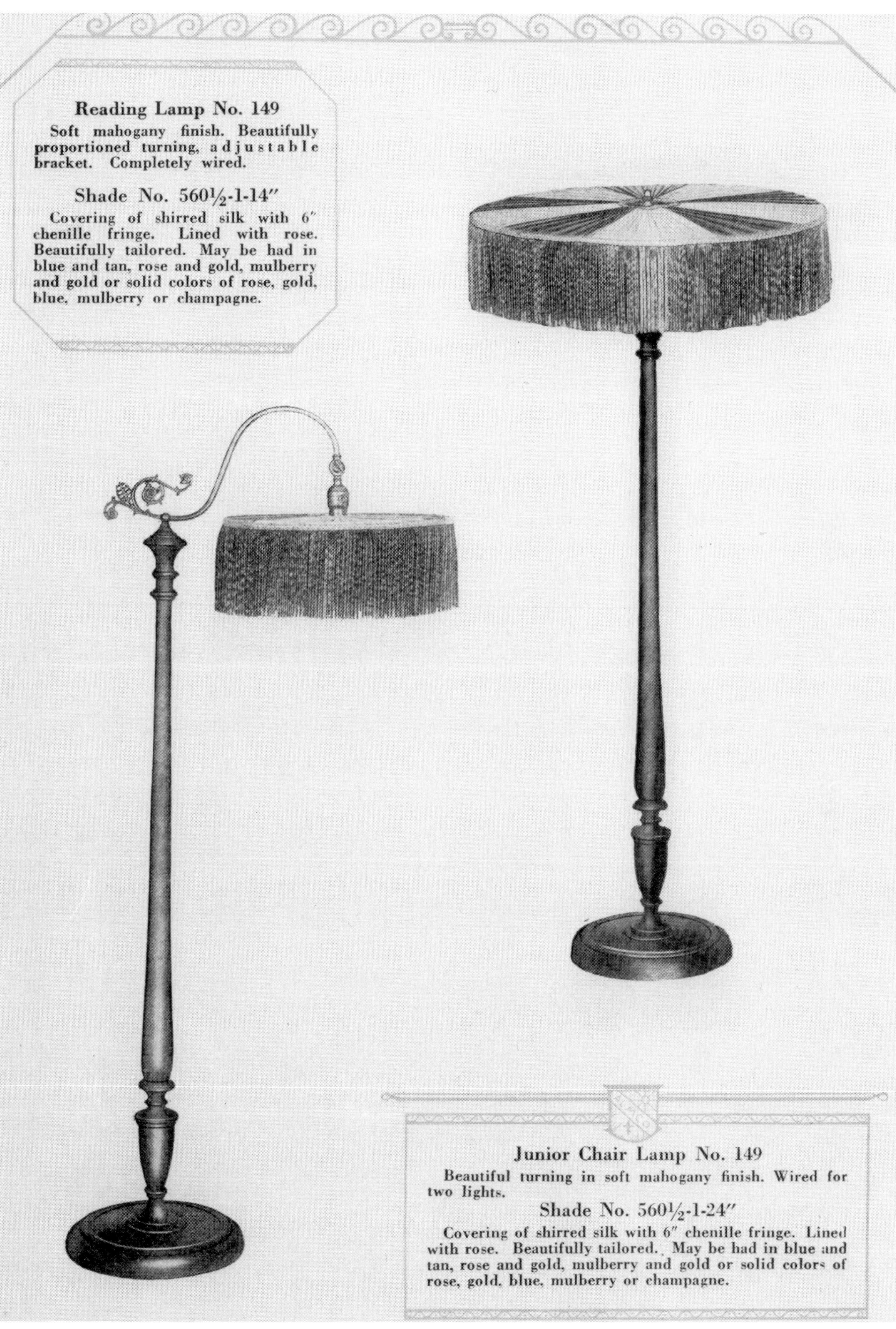

Reading Lamp No. 149

Soft mahogany finish. Beautifully proportioned turning, adjustable bracket. Completely wired.

Shade No. 560½-1-14″

Covering of shirred silk with 6″ chenille fringe. Lined with rose. Beautifully tailored. May be had in blue and tan, rose and gold, mulberry and gold or solid colors of rose, gold, blue, mulberry or champagne.

Junior Chair Lamp No. 149

Beautiful turning in soft mahogany finish. Wired for two lights.

Shade No. 560½-1-24″

Covering of shirred silk with 6″ chenille fringe. Lined with rose. Beautifully tailored. May be had in blue and tan, rose and gold, mulberry and gold or solid colors of rose, gold, blue, mulberry or champagne.

Reading Lamp No. 163
Strictly hand carved with finish of silver polychrome. Adjustable bracket finished to match stand.
Shade No. 363-1-14″
Puffed covering of gold net and figured taffeta. Drum lining and innerlining of pink silk. Dainty rose bud gimp. 6″ blue and champagne tassel fringe over blue silk fringe. Adaptable for chaise longue.
ALMCO
Junior Chair Lamp No. 108
Mahogany finish with shaft covered in blue velour. Interesting turning of Italian origin. Cords and tassels to match.
Shade No. 347-B-24″
Covering of shirred blue georgette. Six inch blue silk fringe and heavy black moss. Lined with champagne silk and innerlining of rose.

Bracket Reading Lamp No. 2520
Brown mahogany finished lamp of unusual design. Adjustable bracket.
Shade No. 41-2-14″
Covering of antique silver lace over burnt orange silk. Delicate silver lace edging. Beautifully tailored.
ALMCO
Semi-Junior Floor Lamp No. 252
Brown mahogany finish. Unusual turning of good proportions.
Shade No. 326-E-26″
Covering of pleated gold silk with champagne drum lining. Antique gold braid galoon and heavy 6″ gold silk fringe. Also made in rose, blue, and mulberry.

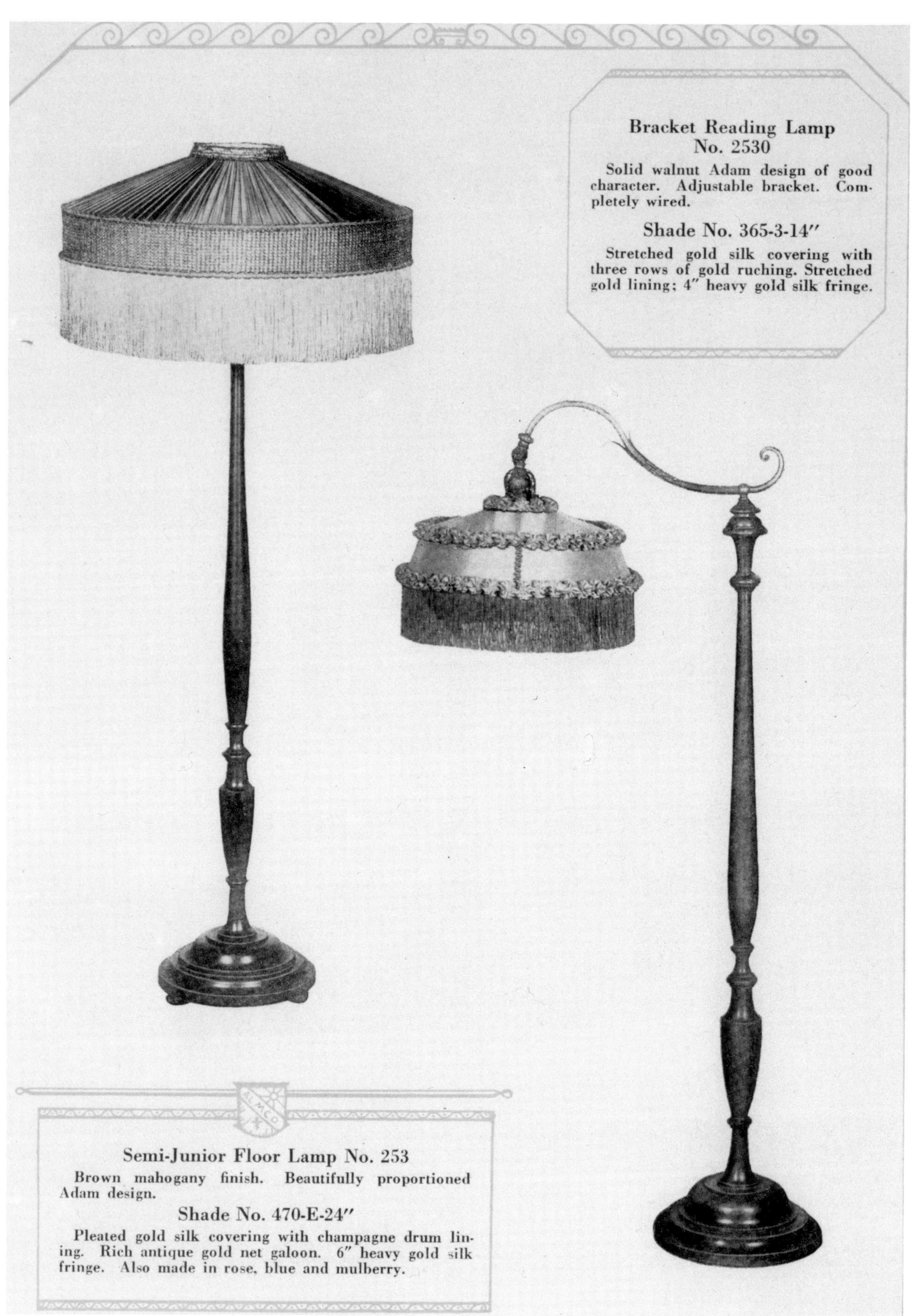

Bracket Reading Lamp No. 2530

Solid walnut Adam design of good character. Adjustable bracket. Completely wired.

Shade No. 365-3-14″

Stretched gold silk covering with three rows of gold ruching. Stretched gold lining; 4″ heavy gold silk fringe.

Semi-Junior Floor Lamp No. 253

Brown mahogany finish. Beautifully proportioned Adam design.

Shade No. 470-E-24″

Pleated gold silk covering with champagne drum lining. Rich antique gold net galoon. 6″ heavy gold silk fringe. Also made in rose, blue and mulberry.

A Leader

An Almco lamp suite you can't go wrong on. It has proven to be the fastest selling lamp we have.

Junior Chair Lamp No. 152

Finished in mahogany. Shaft covered with velour of blue. Cords and tassels to match. Completely wired ready for use.

Shade No. 560-C-24″

Covered in champagne silk with blue strips lined with pure silk. 6″ silk fringe, over silk skirt. Color of fringe to match velour on shaft.

Table Lamp No. 152-T

Mahogany finish with shaft covered in gold velour. Cords and tassels to match. Completely wired.

Shade No. 347-H-20″

Pleated gold georgette covering with gold silk lining and innerlining of of rose. 6″ rose silk fringe and blue tassels.

Davenport Lamp No. 152-D

Finish of dull mahogany. Single light harp fitter. Rose velour covering on shaft.

Shade No. 346-3-14″

Covering of pleated rose georgette with gold silk lining and innerlining of rose. 6″ rose silk fringe and blue tassels.

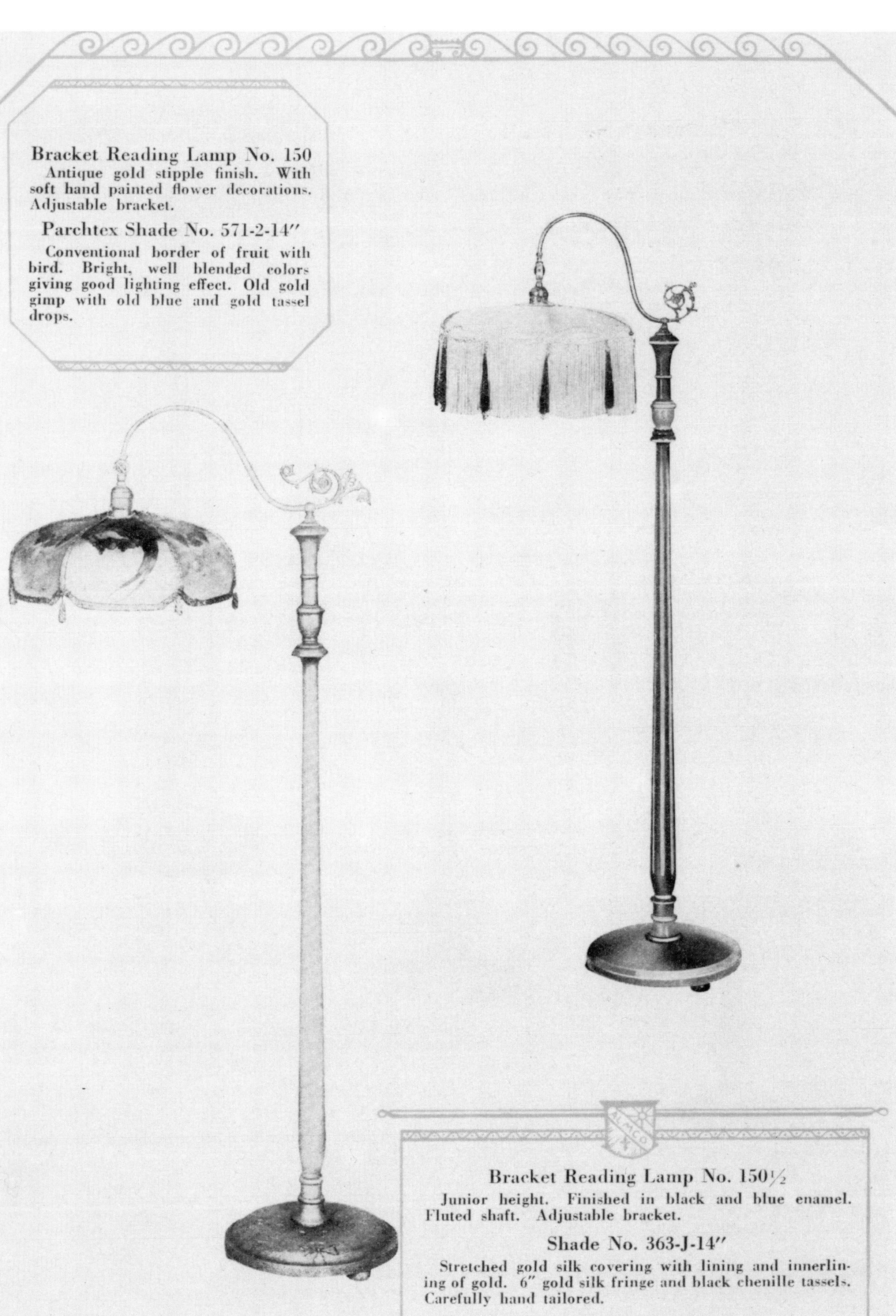

Bracket Reading Lamp No. 150
Antique gold stipple finish. With soft hand painted flower decorations. Adjustable bracket.

Parchtex Shade No. 571-2-14″

Conventional border of fruit with bird. Bright, well blended colors giving good lighting effect. Old gold gimp with old blue and gold tassel drops.

Bracket Reading Lamp No. 150½

Junior height. Finished in black and blue enamel. Fluted shaft. Adjustable bracket.

Shade No. 363-J-14″

Stretched gold silk covering with lining and innerlining of gold. 6″ gold silk fringe and black chenille tassels. Carefully hand tailored.

Reading Bracket Lamp No. 150
Good finish of old stipple ivory and hand painted flowers and stripes in colors to match rose shade. Adjustable bracket.
Shade No. 45-1-14″
Covering of antique silver lace over rose. Puffed rose georgette apron and skirt with silver lace edging. Drum lining and innerlining of rose.
Bracket Reading Lamp No. 150½
Finish of olive green and gold. Fluted shaft with gold stripes. Adjustable bracket.
Skintex Shade No. 570-2-14″
Colonial lady medallion on three panels and plain gold medallion with wreath edge. Roll of old gold lace at top. Gimp of old rose with drop tassels to match.

Table Lamp No. 948

An exquisitively carved and proportioned lamp in the Italian style. Finished in dull antique gold polychrome.

Shade No. 978-2-18″

Shade covered in fuchia taffeta, with lining and innerlining of soft rose silk. Trimmed with puffed gold lace and metal cloth French flower. Beautifully tailored.

Table Lamp No. 949

Strictly hand carved, finished in silver polychrome. A lamp of beautiful proportions.

Shade No. 347-3-20″

Covered with turquoise blue georgette, neatly shirred. Heavy silk lined and interlined: trimmed with heavy silk moss. 6″ silk fringe and fancy two toned silk tassels.

Fibertex Davenport Lamp No. 604½

Finish of antique gold polychrome. A fast selling design. Wired ready for use with single light harp fitter.

Shade No. 560½-1-14″

Covering of shirred silk of rose, gold or blue. 6″ chenille fringe to match. Lined in rose. Beautifully tailored.

Fibertex Davenport Lamp No. 984

Finished in gold or silver polychrome. Twisted fruit design. Wired ready for use with single light harp fitter, cord and plug.

Shade No. 347-S-14″

Stretched champagne covering, with ribs covered with blue strips. 6″ blue silk fringe over champagne skirt. American Beauty lining.

Davenport Lamp No. 208

Strictly hand carved. Finished in antique gold or silver polychrome. Completely wired. Harp fitter.

Shade No. 560-J-14″

Covering of shirred champagne silk. Heavy blue moss and chenille tassels. 6″ champagne fringe over champagne skirt. Lining of stretched champagne, with innerlining of rose.

Fibertex Davenport Lamp No. 988

Interesting design of early Italian scroll flowers finished in gold or silver polychrome. Wired with single light harp fitter and ready for use.

Shade No. 347-H-14″

Covering of shirred grey georgette. Drum lining of grey silk and innerlining of mulberry. 6″ grey silk fringe over mulberry skirt. Mulberry chenille tassels.

Fibertex Table Lamp No. 976

Unusual polychrome finish on gold base. May be had in antique bronze also. Wired ready for use with single harp fitter.

Shade No. 102-2-9″

Covered with turquois blue taffeta with ruffles of silver lace over orchid and gold changeable taffeta. Finished with sprays of French flowers. Blue shirred lining.

Fibertex Davenport Lamp No. 973

Finished in antique gold polychrome, wired with single light harp fitter.

Shade No. 101-1-9″

Covering of burnt orange silk and antique gold lace. Drapes of orchid and gold ribbon strung through lace, with heading of pastel shaded French fruit. Drum lining of burnt orange.

Fibertex Table Lamp No. 972

Finish of antique gold polychrome. Completely wired with single light harp fitter.

Shade No. 104-1-10″

Clover shape shade covered with Fuchia taffeta, shirred with panels of black crossed by antique gold cords. Puffed gold lace top and bottom, strung with rose flower gimp. Drum lining of pure gold silk.

Fibertex Davenport Lamp No. 987

Finished in gold polychrome. Completely wired ready for use. Single light harp fitter.

Shade No. 102-3-9″

Covered with shirred orchid georgette over hand decorated flowers on orchid taffeta. Handsomely finished with silver lace, and French rose sprays interwoven.

Table Lamp No. 28

Finished in mahogany completely wired with one light harp fitter.

Shade No. 458-1-16″

Cover of gold silk pleated. 4″ gold chenille fringe with gold ruching top and bottom. Lined with old rose. Entirely hand tailored.

Table Lamp No. 29

Finished in mahogany completely wired ready for use. Single light harp fitter.

Shade No. 510-1-16″

Shirred gold silk covering with sunburst of mulberry, 4″ gold chenille fringe. Lining of old rose, carefully hand tailored.

Table Lamp No. 29

Big selling design in Mahogany finish. Completely wired. Single light harp fitter.

Shade No. 77-2-18″

Shirred covering of turquois blue georgette. Innerlining of stretched gold and drum lining of American Beauty. Orchid and silver cloth stretched on apron. Wisteria color chenille fringe.

Table Lamp No. 26

Big selling design in Mahogany finish. Completely wired ready for use.

Shade No. P-9-2-16″

Covering of shirred blue silk with rose lining. Tinsel braid and 4″ blue chenille fringe.

Table Lamp No. 934

Strictly hand-carved. Finished in Roman gold and old iron. Wired with 6″ candle and adjustable 2-light fixture.

Shade No. 40-2-14″

Covered in orchid taffeta. Trimmed with French roses and lace handsomely puffed. Lined in silk.

Table Lamp No. 937

Strictly hand carved. Unusual design of Spanish origin. Finished in antique gold and dull black.

Skintex Shade No. 560-1-16″

Oriental design on one piece skintex top. Bright colors, giving effective light. Blue silk ruching top and bottom. A puffed roll of changeable taffeta of blue and gold. Black and gold fringe.

1997 Price Guide to Better Electric Lamps of the 20's & 30's

This book has been compiled from the original catalogs owned by L-W Book Sales. The lamps illustrated within will assure the collector and dealer of the perfect matches on shades and bases. We feel that this book will be a great tool for identifying these lamps. This price guide is of current market values. In some regions of the country the prices will vary. You must remember that this is only a guide and is meant to be used as such. We are not responsible for any losses or gains from selling or buying of these lamps. This is only a price guide to assist you in getting a general idea of the prices.

PAGE 8:
All – **$250+ each**

PAGE 9:
B-58– **$225+**
B-78 – **$200+**

PAGE 10:
B-52,S-1301 – **$300+**
B-53,S-1305 – **$350+**
B-55,S-1302 – **$200+**
B-52,S-1306 – **$200+**

PAGE 11:
All – **$225 each**

PAGE 12:
B-30 - **$125+**
B- 27,S1201-A - **$200+**
B-27,S-1714 - **$300+**

PAGE 13:
All – **$175+ each**

PAGE 14:
All – **$100+ each**

PAGE 15:
B-16 – S-194 – **$4000+**
B-19 – S-192 – **$3200+**

PAGE 16:
B-14 – S-184 – **$3500+**
B-16 – S-197 – **$4000+**

PAGE 17:
B-301 – **$100+ each**
B-307 – **$125+ each**
B-300 – **$75+ each**

PAGE 18:
B-17 – S-188 – **$4200+**
B-17 – S-202 – **$3500+**

PAGE 19:
B-18 – S-190 – **$3500+**
B-17 – S-201 – **$4000+**

PAGE 20:
All – **$3000+ each**

PAGE 21:
B-28 – S-255 – **$3000+**
B-20 – S-166 – **$3500+**

PAGE 22:
All – **$2200+ each**

PAGE 23:
B-305 – S-1253 – **$400+**
B-305 – **$125+**
B-304 – S-1252 – **$400+**
B-304 – **$100+**

PAGE 24:
B-308 – **$200+ each**
B-306 – **$75+ each**
B-303 – **$150+ each**

PAGE 25:
All – **$225+ each**

PAGE 26:
All – **$300+ each**

PAGE 27:
308 – **$200+**
18 S-1 – **$100+**
B-30 – S-1255 – **$125+**
422 – **$200+**

PAGE 28:
All – **$200+ each**

PAGE 29:
B-52 – S-1320 – **$225+**
B-72 – S-1520 – **$200+**
B-57 – S-1321 – **$225+**
B-77 – S-1521 – **$200+**

PAGE 30:
B-51 – S-1323 – **$225+**
B-71 – S-1523 – **$200+**
B-54 – S-1324 – **$225+**
B-74 – S-1516 – **$200+**

PAGE 33:
$2000+

PAGE 34:
$500+

PAGE 35:
$2000+

PAGE 36:
$2500+

PAGE 37:
$2500+

PAGE 38:
All – **$1000+ each**

PAGE 39:
$2500+

PAGE 40:
$2500+

PAGE 41:
$2200+

PAGE 42:
$2200+

PAGE 43:
$2200+

PAGE 44:
$2200+

PAGE 45:
$2200+

PAGE 46:
$2200+

PAGE 47:
All – **$250+ each**

PAGE 48:
All – **$300+ each**

PAGE 49:
All – **$300+**

PAGE 50:
S-1475 1/2 Dec. M– **$200+**
S-1475 1/2 Dec. L – **$200+**
S-1476 1/2 Dec. C – **$1000+**
S-1476 1/2 Dec. A – **$1000+**
S-1476 1/2 Dec. B – **$1000+**

PAGE 51:
All – **$750+**

PAGE 52:
All – **$750+**

PAGE 53:
A-11511/2 – **$500+**
A-11501/2 – **$500+**
A-11551/2 – **$750+**
A-11521/2 – **$750+**

PAGE 54:
$1000+

PAGE 55:
$1000+

PAGE 56:
$1200+

PAGE 57:
$1500+

PAGE 58:
$1500+

PAGE 59:
$1500+

PAGE 60:
S-13361/2-C – **$1300+**
S-13391/2-C – **$1600+**

PAGE 61:
$750+

PAGE 62:
$600+

PAGE 63:
$1000+

PAGE 64:
$1500+

PAGE 65:
$1500+

PAGE 66:
$2000+

PAGE 67:
$2000+

PAGE 68:
$2200+

PAGE 69:
$2200+

PAGE 70:
$2000+

PAGE 71:
$2500+

PAGE 72:
$2500+

PAGE 73:
$2500+

PAGE 74:
$2750+

PAGE 75:
$2750+

PAGE 76:
$400+

PAGE 77:
$400+

PAGE 78:
$400+

PAGE 79:
$400+

PAGE 80:
$2000+

PAGE 81:
$2000+

PAGE 82:
$1800+

PAGE 83:
$2200+

PAGE 84:
$2200+

PAGE 85:
$2200+

PAGE 86:
$2000+

PAGE 87:
$1500+

PAGE 88:
$1500+

PAGE 89:
$900+

PAGE 90:
$1200+

PAGE 91:
$1200+

PAGE 92:
$1300+

PAGE 93:
All – **$250+ each**
EXCEPT
S-13501/2-H – **$750+**
S-13521/2-G – **$750+**

PAGE 95:
7464 – **$100+**
7343 – **$225+**
7466 – **$175+**

PAGE 96:
$200+ each

PAGE 97:
7453 – **$225+**
7452 – **$250+**
7454 – **$200+**

PAGE 98:
7381 – **$200+**
7450 – **$250+**
7359 – **$200+**

PAGE 99:
$200+ each

PAGE 100:
7489 – **$75+ each**
7493 – **$150+ each**

PAGE 101:
7497 – **$350+ each**
7494 – **$125+ each**

PAGE 102:
All – **$200+ each**

PAGE 103:
All – **$200+ each**
PAGE 104:
All – **$200+ each**

PAGE 105:
All – **$200+ each**

PAGE 106:
7419 – **$1400+**
7308 – **$1400+**
7328 – **$1600+**

PAGE 107:
All – **$1000+ each EXCEPT**
7334 – **$400+**

PAGE 108:
All – **$175+ each**

PAGE 109:
All – **$125+ each EXCEPT**
7449 – **$50+**

PAGE 110:
All – **$85+ each**

PAGE 111:
All – **$300+ each**

PAGE 112:
For Reference Only

PAGE 113:
For Reference Only

PAGE 114:
7476 – **$300+**
7475 – **$300+**
7313 – **$50+**
4001 – **$125+**
3890 – **$50+**

PAGE 115:
$200+ each

PAGE 116:
7457 – **$225+**
7459 – **$150+**
7455 – **$225+**

PAGE 117:
All – **$150+**

PAGE 118:
7337 – **$175+**
7458 – **$225+**
7378 – **$150+**

PAGE 120:
108/503 – **$250+**
109/502 – **$250+**
110/501 – **$250+**
Piano Lamp – **$50+**

PAGE 121:
2352/2751 – **$150+**
1493/2851 – **$150+**
2351/1762 – **$150+**
1488/1850 – **$150+**
1397/2357 – **$100+**
1497/2457 – **$100+**
1498/2456 – **$100+**
1398/2356 – **$100+**

PAGE 122:
Floor Lamps All – **$150+**

PAGE 123:
1499/2817 – **$250+**
1399/2713 – **$250+**
1361/2725 – **$150+**
1457/2458 – **$150+**

PAGE 124:
Floor Lamps All – **$150+**

PAGE 125:
1393/1772 – **$150+**
1494/1873 – **$150+**
1475/1871 – **$225+**
1374/1770 – **$225+**

PAGE 126:
1385/1762 – **$150+**
1488/2800 – **$150+**
1476/1890 – **$200+**
1377/1753 – **$200+**

PAGE 127:
1390/1769 – **$225+**
1486/2811 – **$225+**
1346/1766 – **$150+**
1445/1868 – **$150+**

PAGE 128:
1484/2802 – **$250+**
1391/2701 – **$250+**
390/887 – **$225+**
493/876 – **$225+**

PAGE 129:
All – **$75+ each**

PAGE 130:
Modern Table Lamps – **$250+ each**
1312/1727 – **$85+**
1313/1708 – **$85+**
1311/1706 – **$85+**

PAGE 131:
All – **$500+ each**

PAGE 132:
All – **$500+ each**

PAGE 133:
314/589 – **$750+**
400/768 – **$750+**
528/979 – **$500+**
Vanity Lamps – **$50+ each**

PAGE 134:
Boudoir Lamps – **$50+ each**
Modern Table Lamps – **$85+ each**

PAGE 135:
All – **$75+ each**

PAGE 136:
Jewel Case
Boudoir Lamps – **$125+ each**
Set No. 9202 – **$50+ each**
283/685 – **$50+**
284/684 – **$50+**
285/683 – **$50+**

PAGE 137:
Set No. 9352 – **$75+ each**
1200/1605 – **$75+**
220/1604 – **$75+**
219/1603 – **$75+**
Set No. 9264 – **$250+ each**
277/1047 – **$250+**
279/1048 – **$250+**
278/1049 – **$250+**

PAGE 138:
Set No. 9236 – **$200+ each**
222/1610 – **$200+**
222/1609 – **$200+**
222/1611 – **$200+**
Set No. 9351 – **$250+ each**
219/681 – **$200+**
222/679 – **$200+**
236/680 – **$200+**

PAGE 139:
Set No. 9247 – **$200+ each**
1201/1607 – **$300+**
1201/1608 – **$300+**
1201/1606 – **$300+**
237/671 – **$150+**
238/668 – **$150+**
239/672 – **$150+**

PAGE 140:
All – **$150+ each**

PAGE 141:
120/704 – **$125+**
114/514 – **$150+**
1966 – **$75+**
616 – **$50+**
584 – **$50+**
574 – **$50+**

PAGE 142:
All – **$100+ each**

PAGE 143:
6672 – **$4000+**
6668 – **$4000+**
6372 – **$2000+**
6641 – **$5000+**
6519 – **$5000+**

PAGE 144:
$1500+

PAGE 145:
top row
603 – **$125+**
634 – **$150+ each**
7208 (Center top row) – **N/A**
600 – **$150+**
middle row
650 – **$450+**
636 – **$80+**
652 – **$450+**
bottom row
7221 (Book blocs) – **N/A**
649– **$200+**

PAGE 146:
640 – **$225+**
8214 – **$225+**
642 – **$225+**
628 – **$225+**
627 – **$150+**
614 – **$200+**
625 – **$100+**

PAGE 149:
189 – **$100+**
924 – **$100+**
236 – **$75+**

PAGE 150:
All – **$250+ each**

PAGE 151:
919 – **$100+**
2036 – **$200+**
935 – **$100+**

PAGE 152:
All – **$250+ each**

PAGE 153:
All – **$300+ each**

PAGE 154:
All – **$250+ each**

PAGE 155:
All – **$300+ each**

PAGE 156:
All – **$300+ each**

PAGE 157:
928 – **$175+**
240 1/2 – **$250+**

PAGE 158:
274 – **$250+**
164 1/2 – **$200+**

PAGE 159:
Davenport Lamp – **$125+**
Bracket Lamp – **$200+**
Jr. Chair Lamp – **$250+**

PAGE 160:
222 – **$200+**
223 – **$150+**
225 – **$100+**

PAGE 161:
All – **$300+ each**

PAGE 162:
All – **$200+**

PAGE 163:
149 – **$150+**
200 – **$200+**

PAGE 164:
108 – **$200+**
163 – **$150+**

PAGE 165:
2520 – **$150+**
252 – **$200+**

PAGE 166:
All – **$200+ each**

PAGE 167:
All – **$200+ each**

PAGE 168:
All – **$200+ each**

PAGE 169:
All – **$150 each**

PAGE 170:
949 – **$200+**
948 – **$150+**

PAGE 171:
All – **$150+ each**

PAGE 172:
All – **$100+ each**

PAGE 173:
All – **$175+**

PAGE 174:
937 – **$175+**
934 – **$150+**

PAGE 175:
All – **$200+ each**

Table Lamp No. 3012

Sheraton design with mahogany finish.

Shade No. 347-H-20

Covering of pleated gold Georgette. 6″ gold silk fringe. Long chenille tassels. Lining of gold with innerlining of rose silk.

Table Lamp No. 936

Interesting turning of Italian inspiration finished in antique gold stipple. Blue tassels and pull cords.

Shade No. 560-P-20″

Stretched champagne silk covering with strips of blue. 6″ champagne silk fringe over silk skirt. Long blue chenille tassels.

Table Lamp No. 3011

Mahogany finish wired with Benjamin two light cluster.

Shade No. 347-H-20″

Pleated gold Georgette covering with gold lining and rose innerlining. 6″ gold silk fringe over skirt. Chenille tassels.

Table Lamp No. 36

A big seller in mahogany finish.

Shade No. 801-E-20″

Covered in silk, lined with figured cretonne. Silk fringe. Made in rose, gold, blue or mulberry.